Appendix

The following pages have a self-instructional examination you may be able to use to get Continuing Education Units in your state. Please check with your state's licensing department regarding self-study courses before submitting your test for grading. Not all states recognize self-study as a way to fulfill clock hour and continuing education requirements.

States that recognize self-study as o f December 2009

	AL	AR	AZ	CO	CT	FL		
IN	KS	ME	MN	MS	NE	NJ	NV	OK
		OR	PA	TN	TX	VA	WI	

<u>Those fulfilling their CDA requirements may use this course in any state.</u>

Receiving Continuing Education Units and Clock Hours is easy. Make as many copies as needed of the Examination at the back of this book for each individual needing a Certificate. Send one copy per person and $24.00 per person.

You will receive a Certificate of Completion for **8 Clock Hours** and 0.80 Continuing Education Units and your graded examination back for each person for which you have enclosed $24.00.

To pass the examination, you must score 75% or better. There is a $5.00 retake fee per person if needed. However, if you have read the course materials and answered all of the questions, you will do well. We look forward to awarding you with your Certificate of Completion.

You can earn more clock hours using other self-instructional materials by writing to the address below, calling 1 800-23-CHILD or checking www.atiseminars.org.

1

Registration Form for 167 STRATEGIES FOR EXCELLENCE; REACH, TEACH, AND MOTIVATE DIFFICULT AND DEFIANT CHILDREN
8 Clock Hours and 0.80 Continuing Education Units

Number of copies of examinations _____ **(Note: There must be one per person.)**

Name(s) of individual(s) completing examination(s) as you would like it to appear on the certificate(s) (NOTE: Put each individual's name on each examination.)

Please Print

_____   _____

_____   _____

_____   _____

_____   _____

Name of Individual/Center to mail_____

Street_____

City_____ State_____ Zip_____

Number of copies of examination_____ (There must be one per person.)

Amount of money enclosed $_____ ($24.00 per person.)

Pay by check or Master Card____ Visa____ Discover____ Amex ____

Card Number_____Expiration _____

Signature_____

Billing Zip Code _____

MAKE YOUR CHECK PAYABLE TO ATI AND MAIL WITH THIS FORM TO:
ATI/Clock Hours and CEU's
104 Industrial, Suite A Sugar Land, Texas 77478
For further information, or to order books, call 1 800-23-CHILD.

167 STRATEGIES

Name_____

Street_____

City_____State_____ Zip_____

Daytime Phone (_____)_____

Directions: Answer the fill-in questions on the following pages. These questions are designed to help you review what you have learned. You will not be graded on these questions as each child is unique and so is each teacher. However, we will be looking at your answers to make sure **they have been filled in.** You will be **graded on the 25 multiple choice and true and false questions**. Best wishes to you.

Implement 5 strategies you have learned in this book, the date implemented, and the result. Have fun.

STRATEGY	DATE IMPLEMENTED	RESULT

Directions: Choose the best answer to each of the following questions.

_____1. A door opener is:
      a. "I love you."
      b. "Please talk now!"
      c. "Really."
      d. None of the above

_____2. A great way to handle power struggles is:
      a. Startle response
      b. Three positive choices
      c. A song
      d. All of the above

_____3. A strategy for stopping noise in the classroom is:
      a. Silence Sign
      b. Stop and give me 5.
      c. Blurt pad
      d. All of the above

_____4. The guilt-atonement cycle has:
      a. Five Stages
      b. Four Stages
      c. Three Stages
      d. None of the above

_____5. The paradoxical intervention is:
      a. Only used with teenagers and adults
      b. An effective tool for power struggles
      c. A solution for biting
      e. None of the above

Directions: Circle T for True or F for False in each of the following statements.

True   False

T   F   6. Children may misbehave if they are overindulged.

T   F   7. Discipline penalizes misbehaviors.

T   F   8. A power pause is a time when teachers pause before the bell.

T   F   9. The quieter your voice becomes, the quieter the classroom becomes.

T	F	10. When momentum is going, the class is 75 percent on task.
T	F	11. The problem solver approach means, the adult solves the problem.
T	F	12. Students do not need limits to feel secure.
T	F	13. Humans adapt biologically to what is going on rhymically.
T	F	14. The breathing bell is a cue to take three deep breaths.
T	F	15. Children need a predictable schedule and environment.
T	F	16. When you pay attention to negative behaviors, you weaken them.
T	F	17. Stage one of the Guilt Atonement cycle is when the child feels guilty.
T	F	18. Your words make a difference in the lives of kids.
T	F	19. Bright colors on walls can be soothing for the energetic child.
T	F	20. The best way to teach rules is to tell them to children.
T	F	21. Effective consequences are directly related to the act.
T	F	22. It is wise to explain situations ahead of time to children.
T	F	23. The group meeting can be used to discuss kindness and respect.
T	F	24. Have an empty seat at the rear of the classroom.
T	F	25. Have children give you a "wait card" when they are busy.

Choose from 3 Delivery Options

Standard Delivery   Enhanced Delivery   Expedited Delivery

#1) Standard Delivery
• Your paperwork is graded within 10 business days.
• Your certificate(s) will be sent via regular mail within 12 business days from receipt of your paperwork.
• You will receive your certificate(s) in one envelope.
• The grading fee of $3 per clock hour should be enclosed with each test.

#2) Enhanced Delivery
• Your paperwork is graded within 2 business days.
• Your certificate(s) will be sent via regular mail within 5-10 business days from receipt of your paperwork.
• You will receive your certificate(s) in one envelope.
• The grading fee of $3 per clock hour should be enclosed with each test.
• Additional Fee: **$10** for first course plus **$5** per additional course mailed in the same envelope.
Example: Enhanced delivery for 3 courses (1 x $10 = $10) + (2 x $5 = $10.00) Enhanced Fee $20

#3) Expedited Delivery
• Your paperwork must be received by 3pm Central Time for same day grading.
• Your paperwork is graded upon receipt and certificate(s) immediately sent in one UPS envelope overnight.
• You will receive email confirmation of your results.
• The grading fee of $3 per clock hour should be enclosed with each test.
• Additional Fee: **$35** for first course plus **$5** per additional course mailed in the same UPS overnight envelope.
Example: Expedited delivery for 3 courses (1 x $35 = $35) + (2 x $5 = $10.00) Expedited Fee $45

Also Available:
• Fax or email confirming passing grade and certificate date.
• Fee: **$5.00**

Order Form for Enhanced or Expedited Delivery

The $3 per clock hour (per test) grading fee should be enclosed with your test paperwork.
If you require Enhanced or Expedited Delivery, please enclose the appropriate fee along with this form.

Your name: _____ Daytime phone (_____)_____

☐ **Enhanced Delivery**   ☐ **Expedited Delivery**   ☐ **Faxed or emailed confirmation letter**

Payment: ☐ Check   ☐ Money order   ☐ Credit/Debit Card

Check Number _____ Amount $_____

Name on Card _____ Amount to Charge Card $_____

Card#: _____ Exp. Date (Month/Year):_____ Billing Zip Code _____

Signature of Cardholder _____

Are you a past customer? ☐ Yes ☐ No

Fax number (____)_____ Attention_____

Main phone number(____)_____ Email address _____

Fees subject to change after 6/1/2010.

167 Strategies for Excellence

Reach, Teach, and Motivate Difficult and Defiant Children

Dedicated to the memory of my dad, Manny Slomovits, who taught me to care and want to make a difference for others.

167 Strategies for Excellence

Reach, Teach, and Motivate Difficult and Defiant Children

Dr. Maryln Appelbaum

Sugar Land, Texas 77478
1 800-23-CHILD
www.atiseminars.org

Table of Contents

About the Author

Dr. Maryln Appelbaum is well-known as an outstanding authority on effective classroom management. She has graduate degrees in both Psychology and in Education. She has written more than 30 "how to" books including <u>How to Talk to Kids so They will Listen</u>. She has been interviewed on television and radio talk shows and has been quoted in newspapers. She is a leading expert on education and the family. She has extensive experience in the classroom as both a teacher and an administrator working her "magic" on even the most disruptive and difficult children. She is co-founder of the well-known Appelbaum Training Institute, that provides training and professional development across the United States and abroad.

Acknowledgements

I give my sincere gratitude to all the enthusiastic teachers who have implemented these strategies.

Thanks to my son and business partner, Marty Appelbaum, and the entire Appelbaum Training Institute team.

Special thanks to Becky Walters and Kristi Buck Dina at ATi for enthusiastically editing this book.

Introduction

Each child is like a tiny seedling planted deep within the ground of life. The little seedling needs to be watered, fed, and to receive sunlight in order to blossom and grow. It needs a healthy environment, one in which the soil is rich and fertile. It needs just the right amount of caring and nurturing of light and rain. Too much or too little sunlight and water will cause it to wilt. Children are fragile seedlings planted deep within the soil. How they are watered, fed, and cared for will determine how they will grow.

Taking care of children is a sacred task, one that is more important than any other in society. There is no job that can compare with the importance of preparing children for the world. Children are our future. How they are nurtured and guided will determine the adults that they will become. The adults that they become will determine the world that will be. Will children be self-disciplined? Will they be kind? Will they be leaders? Will they have strength and endurance? Will they have courage? Will they be resilient? Will they have good communication skills? Will they have self-control? These are all traits that you can help them to have—with your caring and your love.

Today, there are more than ever before, children who are strong-willed, challenging children, and also more children diagnosed with special needs. This book is designed to help you be more effective with all children.

Do you remember when you first learned to drive a car? There was so much to learn. You had to learn the parts of the car that were relevant to driving: the steering wheel, brakes, turning signals, gas tank, and so much more. You had to practice and practice until you could naturally get into the car and drive. That is how educating children works, too. First, you have to have basic knowledge and skills, and then lots of practice.

Sure you can get into a car without knowledge and practice and drive it away. It will be rocky, but you will be able to drive. You may get into some accidents. You may cause yourself to get hurt. Worse, you may cause others to be hurt.

So too, can you handle children. You can just "drive." But without proper knowledge and practice, it will be rocky. You may accidentally go into reverse, brake too soon, and even put the wrong ingredients into the gas tank. The vehicle that will rock will be more than a machine. It will be the child.

Children deserve more. They deserve for you to know what you are doing. They deserve a steady ride. They deserve to receive a developmentally appropriate environment. They deserve to have bright futures. That is the intent of this book. It is designed to give you the knowledge and skills that you need to do the best you possibly can. It is written to help you to drive with a steady foot. It is the guide for positive discipline.

You deserve to feel successful, to experience the thrill of seeing children step out into the world nurtured and fully successful, and to know that you have played your part well.

This book can totally change your life. Moreover, it can transform your children's lives, too. It will be up to you how much of a change this will be. The more often you read, and the more often you do the exercises, the more effective your learning will be.

Take lots of time to read it thoroughly. Give yourself a chance to absorb what you read. Do each quiz and re-check your answers and make sure you always receive 100 percent. Don't "short-change" yourself or your children.

If you are reading this book, and you are a teacher who is working daily with children, watch the difference as you begin to implement the techniques taught in this book. Share with parents the techniques you will be learning. Invite them to support you by using the same techniques at home. Share this book with them. This book benefits everyone who has children in their care.

Thank you for wanting to learn and grow. You are on your way to learning how to discipline positively.

A Discipline Checklist

Here is a fun exercise for you to check what you know. Quickly go through the statements and mark each one with a "T" for True or an "F" for False. These are topics in which you will become an "EXPERT" by the time you have completed this book.

___ 1. Discipline teaches correct behaviors.

___ 2. Discipline punishes the child.

___3. It is important to believe in the goodness of the child even when the child is exhibiting extremely negative behaviors.

___4. When administering discipline, it is okay for the adult to be frustrated and angry.

___5. After punishment, the child feels secure and has a better understanding of himself and what is expected.

___6. Punishment teaches the child how to deal with feelings.

___ 7. It is important to always use the same discipline technique for all situations so you are consistent.

___ 8. It is not important to be consistent.

___ 9. The child's greatest need is to make his or her own decisions.

___10. There are never too many hugs, too much love, or too much praise that can be given to a child.

___11. When the adult yells, the child knows he/she better listen.

___12. The child will understand discipline better if the adult is really angry when administering discipline.

___13. It is important that the schedule of the child varies according to the needs of the parent.

___14. It is important to praise children even if the praise is not sincere.

___15. Using the word "bad" when talking to a child can cause a child's self-esteem to suffer.

Chapter *1*

THE NEEDS OF CHILDREN

In addition to physical and safety needs, children have very important emotional needs that must be met in order for them to feel loved and secure. When these needs are met appropriately, children behave better, and there are less discipline problems. Pay special attention to these needs if you have a child that appears to need lots of attention. That child most probably has at least one of these needs not being fulfilled. Fill the need and watch the problem disappear.

THE NEED FOR LOVE

Love is a vital force for living (Brazelton & Greenspan, 2001). It can give you the strength to go on no matter what the circumstances are around you. There are songs, books, movies, and plays written about love.

When you feel loved, you feel good all over. You feel like you are important. You are cared about. You feel worthwhile. When you don't feel loved, you feel lonely, isolated, and/or insecure. Worse, you may feel like there is something wrong with you because no one loves you. It is the same with children. They must feel loved to thrive and flourish. They must feel loved to feel worthwhile and capable. Love is always needed, no matter what the age of the person.

Strategy
1

Use Appropriate Physical Touch

There are many ways to show love to children. One way is through appropriate physical touch (Carlson & Nelson, 2006). It's great to get a soft pat on the back, a high five, a warm and caring handshake, or a gentle squeeze on the arm. This is the kind of touch that shows clearly to the child that he or she is cared about.

Use Appropriate Eye Contact

Strategy
2

Another great way to show children they are loved is through eye contact. It has been said that the "eyes are the windows to the soul," and it appears to be true. You can say so very much to children by looking at them lovingly. You can feel so much back by the way that they look at you. Start now to use your eyes to show children you believe in them and that you truly care.

Smile at Children

Strategy
3

Let them know that you are glad to be with them. A smile shows them that you are happy to have them with you. This is a great gift of love to give to children.

Acceptance

Strategy
4

Acceptance is the major way to show children that they are loved (Poole & Church, 2004). Acceptance means accepting all parts of the child, not just parts that you like. The child is a whole package just as you are a whole package. He or she will have good days and poor days. You have those kinds of days, too. You probably want to be loved on the "poor days." Those are the days that everyone needs love even more. So too, do children. Those are the days that you have to make even more of an effort to show children that you care.

Acceptance means never saying that the child is "bad." The word needs to be erased in terms of the child or the child's behavior. When a child is told that he or she is BAD, the child will begin to believe it. The child who believes that he or she is bad, will act the part, will become that way. The only way to switch it off is to believe in the child always, no matter what is going on.

It's not always easy to accept some children. There are times when you may feel frustrated, angry, and even hurt. You can still accept and love the child. You may not be pleased with the child's behaviors, but it is not the child's behaviors that you love. It is the child's essence, the child's individual spirit that is so very individual and unique. This is what you need to nurture and develop. Your goal through acceptance is to help the child to feel loved, and therefore, have less and less inappropriate behaviors.

Instead of telling a child that a behavior is bad, ask for what you want. "I need you to stop running and sit down."

Strategy 5

It's important to not tell the child that his behaviors are "bad." The more often a child hears that he is bad or that his behaviors are bad, the more often the child's self-esteem may be damaged. There is no reason to use words of judgment like "bad." Instead it is more important to tell the child what it is that you do want. For example, when a child misbehaves, tell the child to stop. Tell the child what it is that the child may do. Ask for what you want.

Gratitude

Strategy 6

Use sincere gratitude to show children that they are loved and appreciated.

Statements of Gratitude

"Thank you so very much."
"I'm so glad that you did that."
"That was so neat."
"You made my day!"

Those are statements that can inspire and uplift the child to do more and do better. They are so much better than negative statements that deplete the child's self-worth. The best gratitude is the kind that is spontaneous. It just pours forth from you like a river flooding both you and the child with good feelings. In the beginning, it may take practice at being spontaneous. Say things sincerely. Point out positive characteristics and actions. Point out the specific appropriate behaviors of your children. "Thank you for sharing your lunch with Thomas."

Strategy
7

Say Something Positive Every Day to Each Child

Try to remember to not let any day go by without finding something positive to say to each child at least once. After awhile, you will be pointing out positives more and more easily, and it will become spontaneous. You will see positive changes in the way children behave. Children who have good self-esteem feel worthwhile. They do not need to act out to get attention. They are getting all the attention they need in appropriate ways. Too often, children are told what they do wrong, and never told what they do right. Remember to tell children what they do that is right.

A benefit is that the more positive you are, the more you will see your children being positive, too. They will say positive things to each other.

| Listen and Use Door Openers | Strategy 8 |

A very important way to show children you love them is to listen to them (Appelbaum, 1999). Listen to them when they are feeling good, and also listen to them when they are not feeling good. Listen without judgment to what they have to say. The best way to listen is to simply nod your head and use door openers. Door openers show the child you want to listen and help the child to speak more.

Door Openers
"Really."
"Ahhh."
"Would you like to tell me more?"
"Sounds like that made you angry."
"Sounds like that mad you sad."
"Sounds like that made you happy."

Give Children the Gift of Time

Strategy
9

Another way to show children that you love them is to give them the gift of "time" (Hoffert, 1998). Take time to really enjoy each child. Take time to listen, to love, to laugh, and to cry with your children. This is a world in which people are rushing about trying to achieve dreams, trying to make ends meet, trying to "get it all done." Often, what is omitted, is adults spending time with children, the hope for the future. Children feel this lack. They need you. They need you to spend time with them and help them feel loved and important.

Here is a story to illustrate how the lives of children can be shaped by those who love them, as well as those who also refuse to love them.

Katie lived with her mom. Her mom was exhausted and depressed, and always rushed. She just did not have time for Katie. Katie wanted to sit near her mom and loved when her mom gave her kisses. One evening, Katie's mom told her that there would be no more kisses. She meant what she said. She refused to kiss Katie anymore or hold her. Katie became sad. Katie's teacher saw that she was sad and holding on to a piece of Kleenex that she brought to school daily. Ms. Greene, Katie's teacher, couldn't help but notice that the Kleenex was turning gray, yet Katie continued to carry it. One day when they were alone, Ms. Greene asked Katie why she carried that Kleenex with her. Katie said that her mom used it to blot her lipstick and then threw it in the trash. She picked it up and carried it and put it to her cheek like her mom's kisses.

Katie was a problem teen, getting into all kinds of trouble. She had a hard time focusing in school. She did graduate from high school, and she married young. She and her husband had marital problems and enrolled in counseling. She told the story about the Kleenex in counseling during a session. Her husband was so moved that he got up and gave her a huge kiss. That day marked a turning point for her of feeling loved again.

The moral is that we never know how important our words or actions are and what a difference we can make in kids' lives. Imagine what would have happened to Katie if she would have had a teacher who told her she loved her and showed her how really special she was—who let her talk and express her grief about her mom not kissing her. Imagine if she had a teacher who reassured her and explained to her that it wasn't her fault that her mom didn't want to kiss anymore—that her mom was probably tired and sad about something else. Imagine if she had a teacher who said, "What can we do to help you feel better because you are so important to us?"

You can be that person in your children's lives. You can be the one to show children that they are important and that they are loved.

THE NEED FOR STRUCTURE

Children have a need for structure in their lives that is as strong as their need for love (Cavanaugh, 2006). They need to have structure so that they know what is going on. When their lives are disorderly, they behave the same way. Children are not going to tell you, "I need structure." Their behaviors will probably reflect the opposite. Yet they scream out for it. Take a child on an outing. Bring a new child into the child's environment. Change the time for lunch. Add lots of new materials on shelves. Chaos can erupt. Children need sameness, consistency, and routine.

Their minds are constantly whirling. They are absorbing everything that is happening in their environment. They want to learn everything at once. In the midst of all this natural tumult of growing, they must have a sense of what is going to happen in their lives. This is where you step in with structure.

Routine

There are many ways you can give children structure. Things need to happen at the same time every day. Children need to know that every day at the same time, they will be doing the same thing.

Even the youngest child has this need. A young child who cannot tell time, will still know when lunch is 15 minutes late. Older children know when there is a major change in the way attendance is taken, or their seats are changed. Children at home feel the chaos of divorce, separation, or a new home.

Strategy
11

Introduce New Events Slowly

New events need to be introduced slowly so that children are prepared. They need to be told ahead of time what will happen, and how it will affect them.

Be a Role Model

Strategy
12

Fulfill the need for structure by the way that you act. You are a role model for children at all times. You are teaching even when you wish you were not. They are watching you and copying you (Wallace, 1993). This learning will stick with them longer than learning they get through computers and books.

Be Consistent

Strategy
13

When you say something and do not follow through on what you say, it creates disorder for children (Ruffman, 1999). They need to know that you mean what you say. They need to feel your strength and consistency so that they will learn to have that same strength and consistency.

Strategy
14

Follow Through

When you say to a child, "No," follow through. If you follow through one day, and the next day you waiver, they do not learn about structure. Instead, they are learning another concept, and that is how to get what they want through manipulation. It is important that you do not teach this to your children. The children will never know what to expect, so they will try and try to get something else. The more that you waiver and are inconsistent, the more they will manipulate. The more that they manipulate and get what they want, the more they will think that they can always get what they want from others. This is not preparing them for the real world. They can get what they want in life, but it is from setting goals and learning how to follow through to reach those goals. Teach them to respect you and what you say. Teach them that you do not waiver. Teach them that you do know what you want and that you follow through to get it. Let them learn to respect you. Let them see you as a strong and powerful role model for them.

It takes courage and strength to be

consistent. Most adults worry that children won't like or love them if they are consistent. Being consistent is not the same as being mean. It is instead, an important way to meet children's need for structure. They will respect you even more, even though they seem to rebel. That is because it is a change for them. It is being inconsistent from the way you have been behaving. It will take a little time for them to adjust to your new behavior. They will adjust. They will learn that when you say something, you mean it. Their lives will have structure, and you will have provided it.

Dress Appropriately	Strategy 15

What about you? How do you look? How do you act? Is your own life with children orderly? It is important to look orderly, to take time for yourself each day. If you like the way you look, you will feel better. You will feel more important. You will be showing yourself that you care about you. The children will sense this and have more respect for you.

Strategy
16

| Have an Orderly Environment |

The physical environment of children needs to be orderly, too. Everything needs to have its own special place. When there is a place for everything, children learn exactly where to go to find what they want.

Shelves need to be neat and orderly. Walls and floors need to be attractive and simple. Children need to have order in the general appearance of their environment. Bold and bright colors may add too much energy to an already over-energetic child. Tone everything down. Everything needs to have a clean and simple look that does not distract children from what they are doing.

Storage places also need to be neat. Children learn more from what they see YOU DO, than from what you tell them. Therefore, keep everything neat and tidy, and children will learn to keep everything neat and tidy, too.

THE NEED FOR BOUNDARIES

Boundaries are rules and limits. They teach children specifically what it is that you expect (Greenburg, 2005). They also fulfill children's need for order.

Children need to know the rules. Within those rules, they need to have freedom to "be," to explore. But the basic structure of rules lays the framework for children.

They need to know the areas of the environment that are taboo. They need to know what belongs exclusively to you. They have their own areas that belong to them. This is a rule, a limit, a boundary for children.

Set Rules

Strategy
17

There needs to be some fundamental rules for behavior within the environment (Tanner, Bottoms, & Feagin, 2003). The more you involve children in setting rules, the more likely they are to follow them. Have them help make the rules. Keep the rules positive. For example, instead of saying, "Don't throw trash on the floor," say, "Keep the floors clean." Post the rules somewhere where they can serve as a reminder for children. Have the children help establish a consequence for breaking rules.

Rules are boundaries for behavior. They set limits on what is acceptable and what is not acceptable. The best way to teach rules is to demonstrate them. For example, if you want children to use quiet voices, demonstrate this by using a quiet voice. Have the children practice using quiet voices. Do the same for the rule of walking in the classroom. Demonstrate how to walk. Do it slowly. Have the children take turns practicing it.

THE NEED FOR INVOLVEMENT

Strategy 18

Involve Children

Have you ever gone to stay at a friend's home, and you were not allowed to help at all? You watched while your friend did everything. Your friend thought that she was doing you a favor by not giving you anything to do, but by the fifth day, you were bored and felt useless. That is what can happen to your children if you don't allow them to be involved (Kane, 2005).

Children need to learn to do things

32

for themselves. It makes them feel powerful. Every time they try out something new and master it in their own way, they feel better about themselves. A major key to good self-esteem is an "I can do it!" attitude. That is the attitude of a "winner"—someone who can and will surmount all obstacles to achieve success. That is the attitude that children need to have.

They need choices about things that are happening. For younger children, provide two choices. "Would you like to do _____ or _____? For older children, provide a wider range of choices. It is a self-esteem booster for children to choose from a sampling of books that they will read or learn.

Find ways for children to become involved. They enjoy little jobs and big jobs. Assign jobs each week. These are responsibilities for the children.

THE NEED FOR FUN

Have Fun

Strategy
19

Children have a need for fun. They need to laugh and be silly. They can't be serious all the time. Childhood only comes once. It is a time for fun and games (Wilford, 2006).

It is a joy to be around children. You have the golden opportunity to be like a child yourself having fun with the kids. You will still maintain their respect. You will still be in charge.

There are many children who grow up too soon. Look around, and you will find children who are having to act like adults all the time. Here is a story to illustrate this point.

Stacey was six years old when her parents started treating her like she was an adult. She was very serious. Her parents talked to her as though she were an adult, involving her in all of their day-to-day decisions. She dressed like an adult wearing make-up, jewelry, and the clothing of an adult woman. She was very proud to be dressed like an adult and treated like an adult. When Stacey reached adulthood, she felt that she had missed something very important in her life. She had missed being a child, laughing and playing and acting silly. Because she missed out on this, she didn't know how to play and have fun. She was always serious.

Childhood is a short stretch of life that

can be a joy. It is a time to learn and grow and stretch one's wings. Children need to be allowed to create, to laugh, to play, and to have fun. A child's laughter is like hearing a brook's wonderful spraying sounds. Encourage your children to let go, laugh and play, and be spontaneous. When they say something funny that isn't disruptive, laugh and enjoy their humor.

It will help if you laugh at yourself when you say something funny or when you do something funny. You are the role model, the teacher, the guide for your children.

Have fun.

Here is a quick quiz for you to check to see how much you learned. If there are some areas that are weak for you, re-read that section and take this quiz again when you are through. Mark each statement with a "T" for True or an "F" for False.

___ 1. It is fine to tell a child that she is "bad" when she misbehaves.

___ 2. Children should hear something positive at least once daily.

___ 3. "I believe in you!" is a great statement to say to a child.

___ 4. Acceptance is not as important as involvement.

___ 5. Children need a set schedule each day.

___ 6. It takes courage and strength to be consistent.

___ 7. Bright colors on walls can be soothing for the energetic child.

___ 8. Children copy what they hear the adult say more than what the adult does.

___ 9. Children need an adult who will be in charge.

___10. Rules are ineffective.

___11. There are some areas that children enter because they are "red light" areas.

___12. The best way to teach rules is to tell them to children.

1F; 2T; 3T; 4F; 5T; 6T; 7F; 8F; 9T; 10F; 11F; 12F

The more involved children are, the better they feel about doing what needs to be done.

Chapter *2*

THE REASONS CHILDREN MISBEHAVE

It is important to know why children misbehave. If you can eliminate some of the causes of misbehavior, you will eliminate the need to use discipline. You will provide a happier and calmer environment for children.

BOREDOM

Boredom is the number one cause of misbehavior. Children need stimulation and activity (Kanevsky & Keighley, 2003). Everyone does. Have you ever gone to hear a speaker and felt bored? You may have had the urge to walk out. You may even have had the urge to giggle. You may have started doodling or talking to a friend. You may even have started to fall asleep. It is the same with children. Even more so!

There are some ways you may help children to sit still while you are talking. Here are tips for speaking in such a way that they are never bored.

Strategy
20

Start with Being Enthusiastic

Enthusiasm is infectious (Buffum & Hinman). If you are excited about what you are telling children, it will "rub off" onto them. They will want to listen to you, to hear what it is that you are so excited about.

Strategy
21

Make Eye Contact

That will show them that you are paying attention to them. It will show them that you really care.

Do the Unexpected

Strategy
22

Stand up. Sit back down. Ring a bell. Do something that is completely spontaneous.

Use Props

Strategy
23

Have something visual and concrete that illustrates a point. You can wear a fun hat of a clown when telling a joke. Hold up a magic wand to show that something can happen quickly like magic.

Vary Your Voice Tone

Strategy
24

Speak softly when you are losing their attention. Alternate it with speaking more loudly. Talk faster. Talk slower. Let your voice "speak" for you and set the mood with the tone.

Strategy
25

| Be Dramatic |

Holding the attention of children takes great skill. The more of a "ham" you will let yourself be, the more children will listen. Have fun. Allow yourself to become real serious. Let yourself be sad. Let yourself be happy. You will be teaching children that it is okay to have all of those feelings.

Strategy
26

| Use Gestures |

Move your hands and arms as you talk. Let them speak for you. Use your arms and hands to help you to express all it is that you have to say.

Strategy
27

| Provide Stimulating Learning Opportunities |

Make sure that the learning opportunities are age-appropriate as well as developmentally appropriate. It is important to meet the needs of each child.

Provide Challenging Opportunities

Strategy
28

Children get bored if something is too easy (Passe, J., 1996). They need the challenge of something new and exciting, something that takes some concentration, something that they can master. If it is too easy, they may get the feeling, "Why bother! Anyone can do that."

Provide Opportunities That are Not too Difficult

Strategy
29

Children can get bored if something is too difficult. There is a special frustration of knowing you cannot possibly do something. The attitude then becomes, "Why even try!" When that happens, the children do stop trying. Find the right balance for children. As children master each new learning task, stay "tuned in" to see what they need next.

Strategy
30

| Provide Movement Opportunities |

Have the children get up and move (Armstrong & Rentz, 2002). Have activities that are fun. Have them change their seats. Engage them in a song that all ages enjoy singing.

TRYING OUT NEW BEHAVIORS

It is a normal part of development for children to feel bursts of independence and try out new behaviors. They need to be encouraged and allowed to do this as long as they do not interfere with anyone or anything. They have to be respectful of the rules.

Often children are not told that something is wrong to do. They look at adults as role models and want to copy everything that they do. Here is an example of a first grader. Her name is Hennie.

Hennie has watched her mother putting on make-up since she was a little girl. She sees her mother standing in front of the mirror putting on make-up. She puts on foundation, then powder, then blush. As she puts on each new item of make-up, she's happier and happier. She likes the way she looks. Hennie is standing nearby watching. Mom adds eye shadow, eyeliner, mascara, and smiles at herself in the mirror. Now, she adds lipstick. She has a big smile. She is ready to go out and meet her day.

What about Hennie? She has been standing there watching her mom look happier and happier and prettier and prettier. She sees that it looks like so much fun. The next morning when Mom walks into the bathroom, she sees Hennie sitting on the bathroom counter in front of the mirror putting on her mother's make-up.

Was Hennie misbehaving? Technically, she was; however, it was really about her testing out new behaviors. What about older kids who see someone smoking? They look really cool doing it, so the kids copy them so they can be cool, too.

Teach Children the Difference Between Appropriate Behaviors

Strategy
31

Kids will be kids. They will try out new behaviors. They need to be told which behaviors are allowed and which are inappropriate for them to do.

RELEASE OF FRUSTRATION AND TENSION

Children hold in their feelings and behave inappropriately as a method of releasing feelings of frustration, hurt, and anger. It is difficult to hold in feelings. Here is an example of Bobby and the all too frequent occurrence in young children's lives—divorce.

Bobby senses that something is going on at home between his father and mother. They don't seem happy anymore. They walk around the house looking angry, and they barely speak to each other. When they do speak, they yell. Bobby does not know what is going on. He feels the tension in his home and the frustration. He gets scared. He thinks that he has done "something bad, something wrong." He thinks that he has made his mother and father unhappy. When a child thinks that he or she is bad, the child will start to behave that way. That is exactly what Bobby does. He starts misbehaving.

Reassure Children

Strategy
32

Parents typically want to shield their children so they do not say anything to them when something serious is happening. THIS INCREASES THE PROBLEM. Children are smart. They can feel when something is wrong. They do not need to be told all of the details, but they do need to be reassured that they are not to blame. If there is a divorce, parents need to reassure their children that they had nothing to do with the marriage terminating. Children need to know that they are loved by both of their parents.

There are other similar situations that may cause tension in the home. Perhaps one of the parents is ill and needs surgery and wants to protect the child by keeping it a secret. Perhaps both parents are thinking of a pending move into another city, and are not ready to talk about it. Perhaps one of the parents is concerned about losing a job. Perhaps a parent is an alcoholic or addict. It also could simply be a one-parent household and that parent is exhausted at the end of the day because of all of the responsibilities. All of these are stress areas. The child will sense the stress and has no way to appropriately express the tension, and then may act out.

WEATHER CHANGE

Strategy
33

Prepare Ahead for Changes in the Weather

Anyone who has worked with children for awhile can tell you that children get tense and easily frustrated before the weather changes. Plan ahead on providing lots of movement and lots of opportunities to "let out" the children's pent-up energy.

Not only do children seem more easily frustrated before the weather changes, but the problem is compounded when they have to stay indoors for long periods of time because of bad weather. They have tons of pent-up energy to release. It is frustrating to have to stay inside all of the time. They need lots of movement activities. They need to bring some of the outdoors indoors so they can move around, have fun, and release the pent-up energy they feel.

CHILDREN'S NEEDS NOT BEING MET

Observe Children to Meet Their Need

Strategy 34

Children need to have their needs met in order to thrive. When these needs are not met, children may misbehave (Appelbaum, 1997).

Observe children. Do they feel loved? Is there structure in their lives? Are adults consistent? Are adults following through with what they say to children? Are there wise adults whom the children respect? Do the children have heroes? Do children have someone with whom they can share their feelings? Do the children have boundaries? Do they feel involved and important? Are they having fun? These are all needs that must be met in children.

ALLERGIES

Observe Children for Allergies

Strategy 35

There are children who are sensitive to sugars, dyes, food additives, and high carbohydrate foods. These children will act differently and be much calmer if these foods are eliminated from their diets. Observe the children after they eat. Is there a difference in behavior? If there is a difference, there may be a food sensitivity.

Children can "overdose" on sugar. Children may misbehave after eating ice cream, cake, and cookies. This is one reason that children misbehave more after Halloween or a birthday party. These high sugar foods give the children a lot of energy. When the energy wears off, they become tired and irritable.

There have been documented cases of hyperactive children that were allergic to either foods or airborne substances. When these were eliminated from children's environments, the children became calmer. An allergist can best diagnose this.

FATIGUE

Strategy 36

Observe Children for Symptoms of Fatigue

Children need their rest. Children can become accustomed to going to bed late, but it is not what is best for their bodies and for their development. Tired children are crabby and much less cooperative.

They need consistency in their bedtimes. It is important that on weeknights they go to sleep at the same time each night.

When children go to school tired, they cannot concentrate. It is more difficult for them to learn.

A quiet place in the classroom can be set up for children to go and just "chill out" for a few minutes until they feel more alert. The children go there voluntarily.

HIDDEN MESSAGE TO BOYS THAT "IT IS OKAY TO BE AGGRESSIVE."

Be Careful of Hidden Messages to Boys

Strategy
37

When a boy misbehaves parents frequently say, "Isn't that cute? He's all boy." When they say this, they are unintentionally reinforcing his negative behaviors. The youth then does the same behavior again to get more of this reinforcement. This can be a major cause of negative behavior (Mayeux & Cillessen, 2003). When negative behavior is reinforced for any reason, it increases the likelihood of it occurring again.

CHILD ABUSE

Strategy
38

Observe Children for Signs of Abuse

Children that are abused generally have negative self-images (Maughan & Cicchetti, 2002). They may be angry children who have low self-esteem. Children with poor self-esteem are much more prone to having behavior problems.

The child who has been abused may react in one of two ways. The child may retreat inwardly. This is the child who is the *loner*. This is a child *with walls*. She does not generally like to be touched. She may actually flinch when you attempt to put your arm out to touch her.

Another way that this child may react is to become angry. This anger may be taken out at home or at school. The child projects onto more helpless children what he would like to be able to do to the abuser. This is the child who may be a hitter, pusher, bully, an aggressive child.

This child needs lots of love and

52

patience. This is a child who thinks that he is bad. A child who thinks he is bad, will act the part. Your task will be to change this image by connecting with the child. You will have to move very slowly. Trust will be a major issue. Develop a relationship with the child over time. Reassure the child that you will be there for him. Encourage the child to talk to you. Be a good listener.

OVERINDULGED CHILD

Observe Children for Symptoms of Over-Indulgence

Strategy 39

Parents typically love their children very much and want to give them everything they can. Often these parents want to give children what they themselves did not have when they were children.

This is compounded by the fact that parents generally have less time than in the past. This creates a situation in which parents often feel guilty that they are not spending enough time with their children. As a result, parents try to "make it up" to their children. They do this by providing more and more material items as well as allowing their children to have many privileges.

Often parents set up unreasonable expectations for themselves. When they cannot meet these expectations, they feel guilty and try to make it up to their children. The more they try to make it up to them, the more they give. The more they give, the more the children become demanding. Even two-year olds can behave like little "give me tyrants." Adolescents are even more demanding.

These children come to school expecting their teachers to "wait on them" and give them everything that they want (McIntosh, 1989). When this doesn't happen, they become frustrated and angry. They may have tantrums, become aggressive, hit, push, and threaten to get what they want.

ILLNESS

Observe Children for Symptoms of Illness in Child or Family Member

Strategy
40

When children are ill, they can become cranky. Aches, pains, or fever are taxing on the body. Children cannot always verbalize that they are ill.

Observe children closely. A clue may be a sudden change in behavior. Another clue may be that the child holds or touches a part of the body that he generally does not touch like his ears.

Illness of a close family member is another reason that children can misbehave. Jason's mom was chronically ill. Every time she went to the hospital, he acted out in school. This started in preschool and continued through high school. Children get scared when someone they love is ill. They are afraid they may lose the parent. Often the home may have less structure when a parent is ill. Schedules change, and the primary caretaker changes. The child may become fearful and then angry and act out his frustration and powerlessness.

EMOTIONAL AND BEHAVIORAL DISORDERS

Strategy
41

Observe Children for Symptoms of
Emotional and/or Behavioral Disorders

Emotional or Behavior Disorders (EBD) can occur in children (Rutherford, Mathur, & Schoenfield). When this happens it can aversely affect performance in areas like:

- Self-care
- Social relationships
- Personal adjustment
- Academic progress
- Classroom behavior

Emotional disorders include anxiety and withdrawal. This is characterized by the following: feelings of inferiority and inability to succeed; becoming easily embarrassed; being apprehensive, fearful, excessively shy or bashful; feelings of dread; muscular tension; increased heart rate; and even avoiding anxiety-producing situations (Mash, 2002).

56

Withdrawn children protect themselves from the possibility of criticism, humiliation, and ridicule by distancing themselves from both peers and adults. This self-imposed isolation seems less threatening than social contact.

Withdrawal can keep children from participating in learning and from having friends. It can range from moderate shyness to withdrawing if anyone attempts to make contact. These children often go unnoticed.

Here are some types of anxiety disorders:

SEPARATION ANXIETY DISORDER (SAD)

This is the most common form of anxiety disorder (Bober & Martin, 2006). It is characterized by age-inappropriate, excessive and disabling anxiety about being apart from parents or away from home. School reluctance and school refusal can be a part of SAD. It is very important to reassure children when family members leave that they will be back, most especially if you have children who are exhibiting signs of anxiety.

GENERALIZED ANXIETY DISORDER (GAD)

This is characterized by chronic or exaggerated worry and tension. The child experiences almost constant anticipation of disaster even though nothing seems to provoke it . Worrying is often accompanied by physical symptoms such as trembling, muscle tension, headache, and nausea.

SPECIFIC PHOBIA

A phobia is extreme and disabling fear of specific objects or situations that pose little or no danger (Burnham, Schaefer, & Giesen, 2006). These fears may include animals, heights, or injections. You may see this in your children. There may be some children who are terrified when you bring pets into the classroom. There may be others who are afraid of thunder. Be patient and calming with these children. Their fear is real to them.

SOCIAL PHOBIA

This is characterized by fear of being the focus of attention or of doing something that is embarrassing. Children with social phobia are more likely than other children to be highly emotional, inhibited, sad, and lonely (Higa et al., 2006). They want to be liked by other people but their fear of acting in a way that may invite humiliation is so intense and pervasive that it often leads to loneliness and suffering. It prevents them from forming the very relationships they desire. If other people attempt to push these children into social situations, they may cry, have a tantrum, freeze, or withdraw even further. In the most severe cases, children develop a generalized social phobia. It is very important to be very patient with children who show these symptoms.

OBSESSIVE-COMPULSIVE DISORDER (OCD)

This is characterized by repeated, intrusive, and unwanted thoughts that cause anxiety often accompanied by ritualized behavior to relieve this anxiety. You may see a child doing the same thing over and over again. This repetition creates a sense of security for the child engaging in the ritual.

PANIC DISORDER (PD)

This is characterized by panic attacks, sudden feelings of terror that strike repeatedly, and without warning. Physical symptoms include chest pain, heart palpitations, and shortness of breath, dizziness, or abdominal stress. There is persistent concern about having another attack and the possible implications and consequences (Biederman et al., 2006).

It can be accompanied by agoraphobia. This is anxiety about being in places or situations from which escape might be difficult (or embarrassing), or in which help might not be available in the event of having a panic attack or panic-like symptoms. Common situations include being outside the home or in a crowd of people.

POSTTRAUMATIC STRESS DISORDER (PTSD)

This is characterized by persistent frightening thoughts that occur after undergoing a frightening and traumatic event. Children who have been abused may have PTSD (American Psychiatric Association, 2000).

Here are some ways to help children who have symptoms of anxiety disorders.

Make them feel safe. Provide a safe, caring, and structured environment.
Strategy 42

Do not call on them until they are ready.
Strategy 43

Use praise and positive reinforcement when appropriate, if they can handle it.
Strategy 44

Make the classroom a calm and fun place to be.
Strategy 45

Prevent peers from teasing the children.
Strategy 46

Provide children with alternatives to activities that make them uncomfortable.
Strategy 47

Have the child engage in activities which require minimal participation and gradually increase the student's participation as the child becomes more comfortable.
Strategy 48

Make certain the child has adequate time to perform activities.
Strategy 49

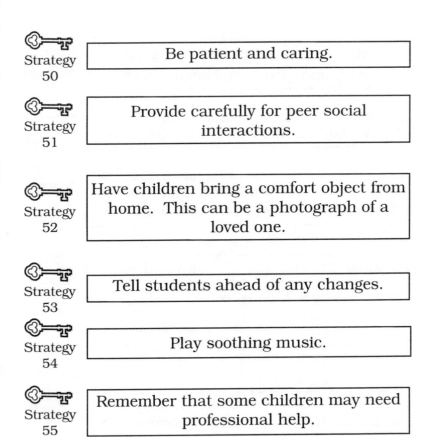

Strategy 50 — Be patient and caring.

Strategy 51 — Provide carefully for peer social interactions.

Strategy 52 — Have children bring a comfort object from home. This can be a photograph of a loved one.

Strategy 53 — Tell students ahead of any changes.

Strategy 54 — Play soothing music.

Strategy 55 — Remember that some children may need professional help.

LEARNING DISORDERS

This is a commonly found problem in children. It is estimated that 50 percent of children have learning disorders. The child with learning disabilities typically has an IQ that is near-average, average, or above average. The child usually has educational problems. They are typically not caused by inadequate educational experiences or cultural factors. It is simply that the child does not acquire and use information efficiently due to some impairment in perception, conceptualization, language, memory, attention, or motor control.

Symptoms of LD
Difficulty paying attention Difficulty with getting and staying organized Difficulty with directions Difficulty with reading and spelling and writing Difficulty with math Difficulty with memory Difficulty with physical education Either very quiet or very active or both

WAYS TO HELP CHILDREN WITH LD

Make sure their emotional basic needs are met. These are the needs already discussed in this book.	 Strategy 56

Strategy
57

Reduce visual distractions. *You will be learning how to create mini "offices" later in this book.*

Strategy
58

Involve the child in choosing topics, songs, activities.

Strategy
59

Build on the child's strengths.

Strategy
60

Allow the child extra time for certain activities because the child may have a slower processing rate.

Strategy
61

Break any assignments into smaller parts.

Strategy
62

Remember, this child learns primarily through discussion.

Strategy
63

Have shorter assignments that involve something difficult for the child.

Strategy
64

Give clear directions.

Break all written assignments into smaller component parts.	⌸— Strategy 65

Help the child with organization.	⌸— Strategy 66

Teach the child social skills.	⌸— Strategy 67

Paint word pictures when teaching.	⌸— Strategy 68

Be proactive.	⌸— Strategy 69

ATTENTION DEFICIT HYPERACTIVITY DISORDER

Attention Deficit Hyperactivity Disorder is a fairly common diagnosis in children. Children are being diagnosed with this at a younger and younger age.

A core deficit in children with ADHD is that they engage in the same behaviors over and over again even when the consequences for the behaviors are negative (Appelbaum, 1999). Thus, they do not learn from their mistakes and keep repeating them over and over again.

ADHD, INATTENTIVE TYPE

These are children who have a problem paying attention. They can be easily distracted. They have a hard time paying attention to details and make careless mistakes. They may not be able to follow directions well. They may lose things like toys, pencils, books, or tools needed for tasks.

Strategy
70

Get Their Attention

Here is what you can do for these students. Start by getting their attention. Once you have their attention, you have to keep it. It means that you have to be especially careful how you handle transitions. This is a time you may lose their attention. Use visuals like task cards to help the students stay on task. Provide cues like hand signals when they are starting to lose interest. Use headphones or earplugs to block out noises in the room.

66

Have a Quiet Area

Strategy
71

It can be helpful for students to have a separate quieter area to sit to do work—a place with no distractions.

Color Code

Strategy
72

Color code everything to help these children stay organized. Color coding items is a great way to separate items. Use different learning centers with different colors. For example, the reading center has little green dots on everything. That way the children know that anything with a green dot goes back to those shelves in the reading center. The shelves are marked so the student knows where to return items.

Be an Edutainer

Strategy
73

Students need you to be entertaining as you teach. They need learning to be fun. Teaching is not as simple as it used to be.

Children watch long hours of television every day, have computer games, and are used to everything happening quickly and in an entertaining way. The more dramatic you are, the more they will listen.

Strategy
74

Use a Dramatic Voice

Have pauses. Raise your voice sometimes and lower your voice other times. Speak quickly at times, and speak much more slowly at other times. Think of funny stories to enliven your teaching. Most importantly, find ways to connect what you teach to what they already know. The more comprehension and connection, the more learning will take place.

ADHD, HYPERACTIVE TYPE

Children with ADHD, Hyperactive Type, are what it says, very hyper (American Psychiatric Association). They get restless, fidget with their hands or feet, or squirm in their chairs. They may even fall out of their chairs. They run, climb, or leave their seat when quiet behavior is expected. They may blurt out questions or answers inappropriately. They have difficulty waiting in line or to take a turn.

Provide Extra Opportunities to Move Around

Strategy 75

Let the child be your helper. Have the child pass out or collect papers, take notes to another teacher, or do a chore like emptying the trash.

ADHD, IMPULSIVE TYPE

These are children who are impulsive. They do things at the spur of the moment (American Psychiatric Association). These children need lots of structure. They need to be told ahead of time of any changes that will occur.

Keep Them Hooked

Strategy 76

It is helpful to make frequent eye contact, encouraging statements, and even pass them little smiley faces or notes on post-it notes.

NEGATIVE BEHAVIORS HAVE BEEN REINFORCED

Children learn to misbehave when their negative behaviors have been reinforced (Valore et al., 2006). Reinforcement may be defined as giving attention to a behavior in such a manner that it increases the likelihood of the behavior reoccurring.

When a child hurts another child, if the adult gives a lot of attention to the negative behavior, there is an increased likelihood of the child hurting another child again just to get the negative attention.

Strategy
77

| Avoid Reinforcing Negative Behaviors |

Words to avoid include: "How could you do this?" "We don't do this in this room."

Here is a story to demonstrate the point of reinforcing negative behaviors. There was a small child named Andrew who constantly tried to get attention from his parents. His parents were never demonstrative with him. They were very involved in their work and in their social lives. They rarely held him or hugged him. Andrew wanted attention. Andrew's need for love and involvement were not being met. Therefore, whenever his parents were talking to each other, he would interrupt. He would pull on his father's shoulder and say over and over, "Daddy, Daddy...." His parents would continue talking and ignore him. The more that they ignored him, the more his negative behaviors increased. His dad finally turned toward him very angry and "smacked him." Just before Andrew started to scream out in pain, he gave a tiny inward smile. He had his negative behaviors reinforced. He had learned that attention of any kind was good. He was grateful for his father's "heavy hand."

This is a sad story. Your job is to make sure that children like Andrew learn to get encouragement for positive behaviors.

MEDIA

This is a media world (Wartella, 2006). Television is a fact of life in most American homes. It is generally on in the background.

Often dinner conversation is replaced with the competitiveness of television programs.

Strategy
78

Limit Media

Studies have been shown that children who watch violence imitate what they see (Ostrov et al., 2006). They become more aggressive. Therefore, it is important to monitor the programs that children watch.

Video games also have the potential to do harm (Grossman & DeGaetano, 1999). Children who grow up learning to "wipe out" characters, are in subtle ways being trained to hurt others.

Monitor carefully what children use and do with media. You are the adult. You are in charge. Look for programs that are non-violent.

The following page has a quick quiz for you to check to see how much you learned. If there are some areas that are weak for you, re-read that section and take this quiz again when you are through. Mark each statement with a "T" for True or an "F" for False.

___ 1. Fatigue is the number one cause of misbehavior.

___ 2. It's important to be enthusiastic with children.

___ 3. It's boring to have something too hard.

___ 4. You can prevent children from trying out new inappropriate behaviors if you tell them ahead the areas that are taboo.

___ 5. When there is tension in the home, the child senses it, and may think he/she caused it.

___ 6. Children can get tense and easily frustrated before the weather changes.

___ 7. When children's needs are not met, they may misbehave.

___ 8. Some children are sensitive to certain foods, dyes, and additives.

___ 9. Sugar is good for children because it gives them the lift that they need.

___10. Television can be linked to aggression in children.

___11. There is only one cause of misbehavior - boredom.

___12. Television does not affect children's behavior.

___13. Parents often feel guilty.

___14. Children who are ill may be more cranky.

___15. The less consistent the adult is, the more the child will act out.

1F; 2T; 3T; 4T; 5T; 6T; 7T; 8T; 9F; 10T; 11F;
12F; 13T; 14T; 15T

Chapter 3

POSITIVE DISCIPLINE

Discipline is very different from punishment, yet often these concepts may be confused (Appelbaum, 1997). See the chart on the following page to understand the differences.

Know the Difference between Discipline and Punishment

Strategy
79

There is a vast difference between the administration of discipline and the administration of punishment. Discipline is used as a tool for teaching correct behaviors. It is a much more positive approach than punishment. Children do not

	Discipline	Punishment
Purpose	To teach correct behaviors	To penalize for misbehavior
Focus	Future	Past or present
Adult's emotion at the time	Patient, firm, calm, caring	Anger, frustration, retaliation, or revenge
Child's emotion at the time	Security, self-control, positive esteem	Guilt, anger, fear, insecurity, thoughts of revenge

have to learn through being penalized. They can instead learn through being firmly, calmly, and patiently taught by the adult new appropriate behaviors. The result is that children will have a greater knowledge of what is expected of them. They will know their limits, and will feel a sense of security because their world is orderly. There is structure. They learn that when they do something inappropriate, there is a consequence. Yet they learn it in a more positive way that does not do damage to the child's internal self.

Positive classroom management is concerned with the future. The focus is not on the misbehavior of the present, but instead on ensuring that the child understands that the inappropriate behavior cannot reoccur in the future. The child learns instead how to behave appropriately in the future. It is a teaching tool.

Punishment has a focus that is completely different from that of positive discipline. It is concerned with behavior that happened in the past. It does not concern itself with building future positive behaviors. It simply is a statement of "I won't tolerate what you did, so I'll show you how mad I am by penalizing you." The adult is frustrated and angry. The child senses the frustration and anger and immediately gets scared and defensive. Thus, the child becomes surrounded by "walls." These are walls that protect the child from being hurt. The child withdraws into this protective walled shell and hears nothing the adult says. The walls can become so thick that the child is buried within these walls in anger. This can become displaced anger with the child hurting others. This can be a child who comes to school and becomes a bully. It may be a child who feels powerless at home, but finds others who are weak who become the victims of this anger.

Other children may start to tell themselves, "I am a bad person." These children may withdraw into themselves and not feel worthy of receiving love.

When punishment is completed, the adult generally feels guilty and may wonder if it was "too strong." The adult may feel so guilty that he then attempts to atone to the child and becomes "too easy," which makes the child more confused. The child loses all sense of the rules and limits.

In still another scenario, the adult may still be angry. He may feel that the child caused him to "lose it!" He may be even more blameful of the child and think of the child as a "bad child." The child can sense this. A child who thinks he is bad, will act the part.

The adult can also become fearful. He may fear what the child will do now to retaliate. This is especially true with older children. The child can sense this fear and will use it to his advantage by acting out even more. The child may become sneaky about misbehaving and passive aggressive. Passive aggressive children do things in such a way that they appear to be innocent even when they are guilty.

| Beware of the Word "Bad" | Strategy 80 |

This book refers several times to the concept of calling a child bad. That is because this is considered of supreme importance. It is vital for the child's emotional development that the child is never labeled "bad." That means she must never be told she is a "bad girl," or "bad student."

It is also important that the child is never told that his behavior is bad. The reason for this is that "we are what we do." For example, you are a parent or teacher reading this book. If someone were to tell you that you are a good person, but that your skills in working with your children were bad, you would feel like a failure. That is because your behavior ultimately is a manifestation of who you are. You are what you do.

You may then wonder what you can say to children? You can say that a behavior was inappropriate. You can focus on what you want the child to do that is correct rather than what the child is doing that is incorrect. You do this by simply telling the child, "I need you to put the toys away and come sit near me." This is **instead of saying**, "How could you make such a mess with those toys? What am I going to do with you? I have told you over and over again not to make a mess."

Strategy
81

Avoid the Guilt Atonement Cycle

This is a very important concept in discipline. Here is how it typically works.

Stage One: The Adult Feels Guilty.

The adult may feel she is not spending enough time with the child. She may feel inadequate in her skills with the child. The child may even be saying to the adult:

- "You are mean."
- "I don't love you anymore."
- "You don't care."

STAGE TWO: THE ADULT ATONES.

The adult tries to make up for her inadequacies. She does this by giving and giving and giving. She gives in when the child makes a demand. She offers things to the child that the child really does not need in order to buy the child's affection.

STAGE THREE: THE CHILD BECOMES MORE DEMANDING.

The more the adult gives, the more the child wants. Nothing is enough. The child may start whining, throw temper tantrums, plead, beg, and behave even more inappropriately to get what he wants. He knows ultimately the adult will give in.

STAGE FOUR: THE ADULT BECOMES RESENTFUL.

The more demanding the child becomes, the more resentful the adult becomes. She thinks to herself, "I am giving,

giving, giving, and giving. All you want is
more and more. I am exhausted. There is
no time left for me. I am always giving."
This resentment grows and grows while the
adult gives and gives, and eventually one
day, the adult gets to the next stage.

STAGE FIVE: EXPLOSION.

The adult explodes. She says
something or does something she wishes she
had not done. Thus the adult now once
again feels guilty and goes back to stage one.

These five stages show the pattern for
inconsistency. It is how adults set the tone
for even more misbehavior with children. It
is vital that adults are consistent with
children.

When children know what to expect,
they feel safe and secure within their
environments. They do not need to test the
limits as much because they know that there
will always be someone to follow through
with them.

The Guilt - Atonement Cycle

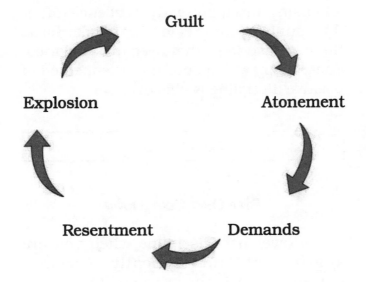

Five Steps Toward Positive Classroom Management

It is easy to talk about being positive and using discipline with excellence rather than punishment. Yet for this to take place, there are five steps that need to be followed. These steps will ensure that the method of positive discipline is effective.

Strategy
82

Cool Down

Step One: Cool Down

Never use discipline when you are angry. It automatically becomes punishment. You can use any of the positive discipline techniques that you will be learning, but if you are angry, it will still be punishment. Why? The reason is that the child may become fearful and/or angry. You will be teaching the child fear and anger for incorrect behaviors. They become fearful or angry because of your strong emotion. Think of the last time that someone corrected you. Was it done patiently and calmly or in anger? If it was done in anger, did you want to listen and follow through? Did you become resentful of the way the person spoke to you even if that person was right?

It is okay for you to become angry. It would be amazing if you never did become angry. It is how you handle your anger that is important. You are a role model at all times for children. They are watching and learning by what you do.

One trick for handling anger is to take a mental time-out—a power pause. Take a deep breath (Rodale, 2006). Think about something peaceful. It can be a vacation place you love. It can be the warm smile of someone you love. Now slowly exhale the anger. Repeat this several times. Each time you inhale, inhale peace and calm and strength. Each time you exhale, release anger and frustration.

Do this until you "sense" all of the anger is dissipated. It is great if you can do it in a place where children can watch you. You will be teaching children this powerful technique to deal with anger. The child will learn that it is okay to be angry and how to cope effectively with anger.

When you are "cooled down," you are ready for the next step in positive discipline.

Strategy
83

Think About an Appropriate Response

STEP TWO: THINK ABOUT AN APPROPRIATE RESPONSE

It is always best to act rather than to react (Curwin & Mendler, 1988). When you are calm, think about the situation that made you angry. Is it something that warrants discipline? Is it something that should be ignored?

Perhaps you have a child that is accustomed to being penalized, a child who thinks that he is bad. It would be better to ignore as much as possible this child's misbehavior and instead, focus on positive behaviors. Focusing on the negative will result in more negative behaviors.

Whatever you focus your attention on will expand.

Perhaps the child was simply trying to get your attention. A child who has his basic needs met, is getting attention. Look at the needs that are not met in this child. Decide if there is a need you can help fill for him?

Look at the environment. Is it developmentally appropriate? Does the child have good self-esteem? Does the child have special needs? Does the child have friends? Does the child need modifications in the environment?

Think, think, and think some more. Look at the family dynamics. Decide which positive discipline technique would be most appropriate for this child at this time. Your goal is to eliminate misbehavior and build a positive self-image in that child.

Collaborate with others. Find appropriate tools to lead this child to succeed.

Choose the Right Time and the Right Setting for Discipline

Strategy
84

STEP THREE: CHOOSE THE RIGHT TIME AND THE RIGHT SETTING FOR DISCIPLINE

It is best to use positive discipline and guidance techniques immediately after the misbehavior has occurred; however, there are times that this may be impossible. If the child misbehaves and immediately becomes scared and defensive, you may have to wait until the child is calm and not frightened. The child cannot HEAR you while the child is upset or terrified. Tell the child that you are waiting for her to "calm down." Be patient and loving, yet firm. Be cautious of frightening the child more. It is important for the child to respect you, not fear you.

Be careful of the setting for discipline and guidance (Laursen, 2003). Make certain that the child does not feel embarrassed. Children are very concerned with what others think. They become embarrassed when disciplined in front of their peers. The older they are, the more embarrassed they become.

Strategy
85

Believe in Yourself

STEP FOUR: BELIEVE IN YOURSELF

Children are smart. They can sense if you are hesitant and uncertain when you speak to them. If you don't believe in your own ability, they won't either! It's that simple. If you are with children, and you have an "I don't think I can do it" attitude, they will know it, and you won't be able to do it. They will take advantage of your lack of confidence.

It is important that children have someone they respect, someone who makes wise decisions (De Montigny & Lacharite, 2005). They need you to believe in yourself. You must believe in yourself. You must begin now to believe that you can handle any situation.

If you believe in yourself, you will automatically talk to your children more confidently, more assertively. You won't be a "wimp." You won't be a doormat. You will speak confidently. You won't lose your temper. Your children can sense in your voice and in your posture whether or not you are feeling strong in what you are saying. They "intuitively" feel whether or not you believe in yourself, whether you believe that you can succeed. If they feel your confidence, they will listen to you.

It takes a shift in attitude. Your attitude has to be, "I can handle any situation. I can do it!" This book can teach you all the best techniques, but it cannot change your attitude. Only you can do that. Only you can turn yourself into a more positive and confident person.

You must do it. You must believe in yourself. That is the key to having your children believe in you. That is the key to respect. Think of people you know who are confident. They believe in themselves. It doesn't matter whether or not you believe in them. They are happy and fulfilled people and much more confident with their abilities. They know "they can do it" and therefore they DO IT.

Now is the time to turn your attitude around. Believe in yourself. You can do it.

Strategy
86

Believe in the Child

STEP FIVE: BELIEVE IN THE CHILD

Children need to have someone who believes in them (Tipps, 2006). They need to have someone in their lives, someone who accepts them and sees beyond any behaviors to their essential goodness, uniqueness, and strength. If you can see these traits in children, they will begin to see them, too.

A child is so much more than behaviors. Each child has a unique and special personality. This personality that you see, often gets stifled and colored by the expectations and beliefs of others. Sometimes, this personality hurts. Hurts can easily be covered up with misbehaviors or through retreating within a shell.

Think of a caterpillar coming out of the cocoon. It struggles and struggles and finally emerges into a butterfly. So too can children struggle because of things that have happened to them in their lives. You cannot see the hurts, but that does not mean they are not there.

Children are fragile. They need to be nurtured. They need to be believed in. The more you believe in the child, the more "good" the child will see. You will see a change in behavior that will amaze you.

This may take a shift in attitude within you. It means nurturing and believing in the child whom you have not believed in before. It's easy to believe in the child that does everything right. But what about the child who can't seem to do anything right? What about the rebellious child—the challenging child? That is the child that needs your love and your belief the most. That is the child in whose life you can make the biggest difference.

Billy was a child who always got mediocre grades. Everyone thought that he was a mediocre student. His family and his teachers all thought this was true. Even Billy thought so. Finally, when Billy was in high school he had a teacher who said to him, "You can do better." No one had ever said those words to him before. Now he had someone who believed in him, someone who believed that he could and would do better. He did! He started getting all A's and B's. Today, he is a successful international financial consultant. This is because of the power of someone who believed in him. One teacher changed his whole life.

Mary was emotionally and physically abused at home. She acted out at school and in public. Mary screamed out for attention because she didn't feel loved. Her Aunt Jessica moved near by. Aunt Jessica believed in Mary. She believed that Mary could do and achieve anything. Aunt Jessica saw through Mary's "badness" to the little hurting girl who simply needed love and someone to believe in her. Mary completely changed. She started taking pride in herself. She started walking with confidence and talking with enthusiasm. Mary went to college and became a social worker helping other people. This was all because of one person who believed in her.

Here is another story to illustrate this

point, a story about a teacher who made a difference - Miss Dover.

***

I was burned-out , and it was only my first year teaching fourth grade when Jenny Lee Williams came into my already crowded classroom one day in late fall. She wore the same outfit every day, a pair of brownish stained pants and a t-shirt that once was white, but now was grey. Her hair was uncombed, dirty and unevenly cut. She had huge dark and sad eyes. She quietly sat at the back of the room. Her homework was turned in on wrinkled, erased paper each day and had many errors. She seemed to have no friends.

There was something about her that made me want to know more. I spoke to other teachers and looked at her past school records. I found out that Jenny Lee had done well in kindergarten, but then had steadily declined in school to the point where she now appeared to be a slow learner. Her mom got sick when she was in first grade, and Jenny's little life seemed to fall apart. Her dad started drinking. By second grade, her mom was in the hospital most of the time, critically ill, and her dad had been arrested for drunk driving. Jenny Lee's grandmother was living with them to help out. By third grade, Jenny was doing worse and worse in school. Her mom passed away, and her dad was in a rehabilitation center. Jenny lived with her grandmother.

Now Jenny was in my class, unmotivated, sad, and behind in her work. I was not convinced that Jenny was a slow learner. There was something about Jenny that reminded me of my own daughter that I had lost last year. I think it was those big dark eyes. I decided I would strive to give Jenny whatever I could to get her back on target.   The first thing I did was set up a time when we could meet. I asked her to meet me after school.

I told her that I saw from her work that she had potential. Jenny told me that she always had wanted to be a news anchorwoman; finding stories and reporting them on television. Now she really didn't feel like it anymore. I said, "Let's just start with today and work on getting you caught up. We'll take it one day at a time." She wasn't enthused. I invited her to come back to meet with me after school, and she agreed. Soon she was coming several times a week.

At that time, 3:00 p.m. became the highlight of my day. When Jenny finally smiled that sweet shy smile, after mastering a really tough problem, I felt my heart burst with joy.

Before the winter holiday, kids usually bring gifts. I knew Jenny had no money so I really didn't expect anything from her. She came the last day before winter break with a brown paper bag. She had written on the bag, "To Miss Dover—Happy Holidays. Thank you, Jenny." There was a big smiley face right next to her signature. I opened the bag and inside was a 2 inch by 3 inch magnetic saying. It said, "I'll always remember you."

I was very touched. I said, "Thank you so much, Jenny. It's beautiful." She got real quiet and said, "I gave it to my mom right before she died. She had it next to her hospital bed so she could see it every day. She's now living in my heart so I'll always remember her. I wanted you to have it now because I'll always remember you, too, Miss Dover. You gave me back something I was missing. I have hope." We both cried a few tears. I told her about my Lizzy, who was gone too, and how Jenny gave me back something too, and I would always remember her.

The following summer, Jenny moved. Her dad came home, and they started a new life in a new neighborhood. I missed Jenny's sweet smile and felt great joy when I received cards from her several times a year. The cards always started out with the same four words, "I'll always remember you." My favorite cards were the ones that came each year on Mother's Day and said, "To a Special Friend". She signed the cards, "I'll always remember you."

When Jenny was eighteen, she sent me an announcement of her high school graduation. She was named, "Most Likely to Succeed." I went with joy and pride to see her beaming face. When she graduated college, she sent me an invitation to watch her graduate with a degree in journalism. Of course, I proudly went. I not only saw her graduate, but I got to meet her boyfriend Alex.

When she and Alex got married, she asked if I would come to her wedding, where she reserved a seat for me in the front row. When she wrote her first story, it was about kids and depression. She dedicated that story to me on national TV saying, "To Miss Dover, I'll always remember you. You gave me hope."

And so today, after 32 years of teaching, I, too, always remember Jenny Lee Williams. I still have that little magnetic saying. I put it in a frame by my bed so I see it first thing every morning and last thing every night. I'll always remember the child who showed me that I could make a difference. She opened my heart back up to love. She gave me the gift of hope for all children and hope for myself, to keep striving to help each child. After all, that is what teaching is all about - giving hope, helping children.

.

Can one person make a difference? You bet! Believe in the child and you and the child together can reach for stars.

You can do this for your children too. Believe in them, and they will soon begin to believe in themselves. You will have helped make this a better world for children.

SUMMARY

Following these five steps toward positive classroom management will completely change the way that you and your children relate. These are the foundation for not only effective discipline, but for more effective living.

You will teach children how to deal with anger when you "cool down," when you take time to act rather than to react. Children will trust you more because you are careful to choose the right setting and the right time for discipline. Your belief in yourself will provide them with a strong sense of security as well as give them respect for you. Most importantly, your belief in children will give them what they need most to function in the world. You will remind them of the good that they can achieve, and help them to reach their highest potentials.

In turn, you will benefit also. You will become strengthened each time you use these five steps. You will believe more and more in yourself, your abilities, and your own strengths.

Self Quiz

Mark each statement with a "T" for True or an "F" for False.

___ 1. Discipline with excellence focuses on the misbehavior of the past.

___ 2. The adult's emotion during discipline is anger and frustration.

___ 3. The child feels secure, and learns self-control and understanding when discipline is administered.

___ 4. It's okay to feel angry and discipline your child.

___ 5. "Cool down" is step one toward positive discipline.

___ 6. It is better to act rather than to react.

___ 7. There are seven steps in the Guilt-Amendment Cycle.

___ 8. It is important that the child repsects you, not fear you.

___ 9. Embarrassment is an effective discipline tool and should be used as frequently as possible.

___ 10. Your attitude has to be, "I can handle any situation."

___ 11. It's better to spend your time believing in the child who rarely misbehaves, who does everything right.

___ 12. Children need to have someone in their lives who accepts them and who sees beyond any misbehaviors.

1F; 2F; 3T; 4F; 5T; 6T; 7F; 8T; 9F; 10T; 11F; 12T

Chapter 4

POSITIVE CLASSROOM MANAGEMENT

"Do something, and when you have done something, if it works, do it some more, and if it doesn't work, do something else."

Franklin Delano Roosevelt, (1932)

This is a quote by Franklin Delano Roosevelt from the 1932 Baltimore Address. That quote is as relevant today for discipline as it was in his day with the subject matter he was talking about.

There are no magic discipline

techniques that can be used over and over again that always work. What works one time with one child may not work again. What works for one child may not work for another child. Therefore, you need to have a variety of discipline techniques to handle all situations.

This chapter is designed to give you a large sampling of techniques to help you with children. The more often you read them, the more familiar you will become with them, and the easier it will be for you to find the most perfect discipline solution when you need it.

Some are very simple. Some may be ones with which you are familiar. That is fine. Those can simply be a reminder for you. Others will be brand new. Have fun learning effective solutions to use with the children.

Strategy
87

Go to Child

If you shout across the room at a child, you are teaching the child to YELL through role modeling. When the child is misbehaving in another room or in another part of the same room, walk over to the child. Get down on the child's level and look at the child (Anguiaro, 2001). Quietly and firmly tell the child *not what he is doing wrong,* but what it is that *you want.*

Look into the child's eyes, and make sure the child is looking at you.* Most children don't want to make eye contact because they think they can pretend that they didn't hear you if they are not looking at you. If one of the children looks away when you are looking at him, say very quietly and firmly, "I know that you can hear what I am saying."

*If there is a cultural difference, and the child has learned to avoid eye contact, it is important to not make the child look at your eyes. Be close to the child when speaking. Look directly at the child, but do not make eye contact. State calmly and confidently, what it is you need to have the child do.

Omit the Word "Don't"

Strategy 88

When you say the word "don't" followed by a verb, children hear the verb. They generally pay no attention to the word "Don't" and just do the action verb. For example, when a child hears, "Don't run," the child typically continues to run. When a child hears, "Don't yell," the child typically continues to yell.

Instead say what it is you really want to have occur. Use the action verb. Say, "Walk, " "Talk quietly."

Strategy
89

Redirect the Child

Often children who are mischievous simply need to be redirected toward another activity (Silsbee, D., 2005). This is the positive approach. It will help you avoid words like "no" and "don't." A child who hears "no" and "don't" over and over again, will start to say those words.

Example
Jason is getting that look that can mean he is going to hurt someone. You could say, "No." However, it is better to say: "Jason, I need you to run an errand for me."

Here is another example. Miss Thomison has a student named Danny in her classroom. Danny moves near two other students working together. Miss Thomison knows from past experience that Danny will probably start teasing the other two students. She says, "Danny, I need you to help me." She has redirected Danny's behavior and avoided any negative statements that would lower Danny's self-esteem.

It is perfectly okay to come up with something else for the child to do to divert him from misbehavior. Give the child something more fun and more stimulating. The child may have been bored, and that may be why he was misbehaving.

Other times you will find that the child is really "trying to tell you something" with the misbehavior. It could be that something is either too easy or too difficult. In either case, the child can become defiant or bored and not want to engage in the activity. Be an observer.

Quiet Voice

Strategy
90

This is a very simple technique. The quieter your voice becomes, the quieter children will be (Curwin & Mendler). Often adults yell to get children's attention. The opposite is true. The lower the adult speaks, the quieter children become. Conversely, the louder the adult's voice, the louder children become.

If you have a day in which you have laryngitis, you will probably notice that the children use lower voices. They adjust to accommodate you. If you want to get a child's attention, get down to the child's level and whisper to the child. Most typically, the child will stop doing whatever he is doing, in order to better hear you.

Strategy
91

Laughter

Sometimes, a child's behavior is genuinely funny. Think about it. It's amazing what children can come up with. It's totally incredible. Some situations that occur with children are as hilarious as any comedy television program.

Have fun (Schwarz, G., 1989). Enjoy yourself. Laugh with children rather than get angry. Your laughter needs to be genuine and fun. It can't be sarcastic. The child can't interpret it as making fun of him.

Instead the child needs to see that you are simply enjoying the uniqueness of the situation.

| Consequences | Strategy 92 |

A consequence is the direct result of a misbehavior. For consequences to be effective, it is best for them to be related to the act (Curwin & Mendler). For example, if a child makes a mess, the logical consequence is for that child to clean it up. It may take a little longer and may not be as good of a job as you would have done, but the child will have learned to be responsible for her behavior.

It's important to be patient when using this technique. Children work at a slower pace, so it will take longer for them than it would for you to follow through. Gently encourage children along the way, especially if it's a long and difficult situation to fix.

Children need to be told ahead of time if there will be a consequence for their misbehavior. "Jamie, if you do not return your book to the shelf, you will not be allowed to take out other books." The child then knows what to expect.

Too often, there are absolutely no

consequences for misbehavior. The world has consequences for misbehavior. When a person goes through a traffic light, the person will get a ticket. Consequences prepare the child for the world.

Remember that children won't change their behavior unless it creates a problem for them. Typically, the child is not having the problem. It is the adult who is having the problem. The child may be having a great time engaging in the misbehavior.

Examples
If the child won't put away something he has used, he cannot get out the next thing until the first thing is put away.
If the child tears or breaks something, the child has to repair it or earn the money to fix it.

Whenever possible, involve the child in coming up with consequences. You may have to act out reverse roles so that the child can really see what has happened.

The goal of a consequence is not to punish, but to teach the child to be responsible for his actions. Be cautious of the way you speak to the child so that your voice is caring, yet firm so that the child knows that you will FOLLOW THROUGH.

Remember to give approval when the job is complete. Praise and positive reinforcement are effective techniques for increasing the likelihood of positive behaviors recurring.

Group Meeting

Strategy
93

The group meeting is a powerful bonding tool (Frederickson et al., 2005). It needs to be held at least weekly. The group sits together and has fun. An atmosphere of safety and trust are established. When there is a discipline situation, it can be discussed as a group. Focus the group's attention on how you want the class to be outstanding. It is your wish that everyone treats each other with respect and kindness. Discuss kindness and respect and how they are shown.

Have the group discuss discipline situations and come up with solutions. For example, there may be too much noise. Ask the group to come up with ways to have it be quieter. Once again, the more they are involved, the more likely they are to follow through. This technique works for children of all ages.

Strategy
94

Overlook Negative Behaviors/ Encourage Positive Behaviors

This is the easiest technique of all but it can be the most difficult to do. The reason for this is that it calls for INACTION when there is some misbehavior.

Often a child misbehaves because he has learned that it is one sure way of getting attention. This is a negative form of behavior that the child has learned. The child becomes accustomed to engaging in the negative behavior and then getting reinforcement (negative attention) for it.

This is particularly true of the child who thinks that he is "bad." This child is accustomed to engaging in negative behaviors and constantly getting reinforced (negative attention) for these behaviors. You can end the cycle by ignoring these behaviors whenever possible. When you pay attention to these negative behaviors, you are inadvertently reinforcing the child's belief that he is "bad." You are reinforcing the child's faults rather than his strengths.

Find the positive strengths in your children. Sincerely praise these strengths. This will enhance your children's self-esteem.

This does not mean ignoring all misbehavior, especially if a situation is dangerous. This is an effective technique for reversing a pattern. Some misbehaviors need other techniques. That is why this book is filled with different strategies and solutions. Use your judgment as to which will work best.

Here is an example in which this would be effective. Johnny continually blurts out in class. This is a chronic problem. His teacher is annoyed and actually expects this negative behavior from Johnny.

When he does it, she says, "Johnny, stop that now!" "Johnny, again!!!!" "Johnny, what have I told you before over and over again about talking out in class?" The negative behavior of Johnny blurting out is being reinforced with lots of attention. The behavior increases daily. Instead, the behavior needs to be ignored and Johnny needs to be re-directed to more apprpriate behavior.

Use the Momentum Technique

When momentum is going, the class is 95-100 percent on task. When momentum is lost, the class is 0 percent on task.

Keep your eyes moving. Eye contact is your most powerful tool in maintaining classroom control. It is the single best intervention for preventing 95 percent of classroom misbehavior.

Misbehaviors can be nipped in the bud through timely, direct eye contact. Keep your eyes moving to scan the entire room at least once every minute. Focus upon clusters of four or five students at a time. Hold that gaze for 4-5 seconds and then move on to another group.

Most teachers have less eye contact with students sitting in the furthest corners of the room, and that is where most misbehavior occurs. Walk around and make eye contact (Belifiore et al., 2002).

Headphones

There are some children who simply cannot handle noise. These children can benefit from having a set of headphones. The headphones are not connected to anything. The child wears them to block out noise. The child only uses them when needed.

Have a Relaxation Station

This is an excellent technique for teaching children to relax when they are upset. You will need to set up a place that is calming. It can have a small pillow, a few books, headphones, and a soft calming picture or a photograph on the wall. The child goes there when she needs to "cool down."

Introduce this station by explaining that there may be times when children may get angry, sad, or confused. That is when the "relaxation station" is a good place to go (Prestia, 2004).

You can have a special timer for the child to limit the amount of time spent in the relaxation station. A liquid timer works well.

When the child comes out of the relaxation station, it's important to redirect the child to do something apprpopriate.

Strategy 98

Use Offices

Provide offices by combining two file folders. The children decorate the outside of the "office."

Strategy 99

Have a Rocking Chair

Rocking is calming. Have a rocking chair in a separate area of the room or have it in the relaxation station.

Strategy 100

Have an Empty Seat

Have an extra empty seat at the front of the classroom. When a child is having a bad day, have the child move to the empty seat. Keep it simple. Calmly tell the child to move to the seat. "Johnny, I need you to move to this seat for right now. Thank you." Then go on with what you were doing.

Strategy 101

Use the Problem Solver Approach

This is a technique to use when you have tried other techniques first, and they have not been successful. Tell the child honestly. "I have a problem. I have tried to have you stop doing _____, and it has not worked. I have tried everything that I know how to do. I need your help. I need you to come up with a way for you to remember NEVER EVER to do _____ again." Give the child a chance to come up with her own solution to this problem.

If she comes up with something too easy, say, "That's a good start. I can see you have been thinking about it. I need you to come up with something that will really ensure that you remember not to do _____ again."

If the child comes up with something too difficult to remember to do, say, "Wow, you are really working hard at this. Thank you. That one may be a little too difficult. Do you have something a little easier on yourself that will still work?"

This is a powerful technique because it empowers the child to come up with the solutions. The more children are involved, the more likely that they will follow through.

| Use Wait Cards | Strategy 102 |

When a student wants a teacher's attention, the child often yells out, "Teacher,

teacher!" This can interrupt the entire class. You need a way to show the child that you will pay attention to that child. You simply can't do it right then. Explain ahead of time that this card means that you will address the child's needs as soon as you are able to do so.

Strategy
103

Use Behavior Notes

When students are doing great, it is good to let them know. This is especially true for students who rarely hear kind words. It is a great way of calling attention to positive behavior. Carry in a pocket a packet of post-it notes. When you see a student who is normally loud being quiet, or a student who is typically out of his seat, sitting quietly in his seat, give the child a Behavior Note. Take the sticky note and draw a smiley face or write words like, "Good job." Post it on the student's desk or near the student so he can see it.

Strategy
104

Acknowledge Student Leaders

This is a powerful technique. It is reserved for the child who "seems to want to take over." This is a student who other children admire and imitate.

Using this technique, you acknowledge the child's leadership role and invite the child to cooperate with you in becoming an even more effective leader.

Talk to the child and acknowledge how powerful he is. Explain that you believe the child has leadership abilities. Tell the student that you would like to help him develop these abilities. It's important that you are sincere. If the child is usurping your authority and your leadership, the child truly does have leadership abilities; however, they are currently channeled in a negative direction. These abilities simply have to be channeled into more positive directions. That is what this technique will do.

You and the child jointly work out a plan to develop these leadership abilities. Have times and situations in which the student will be in charge. The only hitch is that the child will have to use his leadership ability to help other students also follow classroom procedures. The child has to become a role model for others on how to act within the framework of the classroom.

Have fun together. This is a great technique. You will both be empowered and get closer through its use.

Strategy 105

Teach Appropriate Substitute Words for Inappropriate Language

Kids use inappropriate language, profanity, for the following reasons. They hear it at home and sometimes don't even know what it means. They may use it to distract the person from what they are arguing about. They may even use it to upset the other person, and they may use it as a "learned" expression of anger.

When younger children use inappropriate language, they often do not know there is anything wrong with the words when they first say them. It is the reaction of adults that will actually reinforce the behavior. If an adult is shocked and says something like, "We don't ever say those words," the adult is calling attention to the misbehavior. The more attention the adult gives the words, the more the words will be reinforced.

The first few times you hear the word, simply do nothing. Remember, the more appalled you are, the more you are reinforcing the behavior. If the child continually uses inappropriate language, tell the child calmly, that the child may not use that word in your presence. Be calm. Use words like, "You may not say that word in our class. Speak slowly and calmly and firmly. If it still continues, which it may, use the following technique. This is very effective with children through elementary school. Simply tell the child, "I can see that you like saying that word over and over. You can't say that word in my classroom. However, you can choose a word to say that I WILL APPROVE OF to say when you feel like saying the other word. If you forget the new word, I will remind you." If the child does forget, calmly remind the child to use the new word.

Use Traffic Light Cards

Strategy
106

This is a simple way of teaching boundaries. Explain to the children that just like in traffic, there are lights, so too, will there be traffic lights in your room. Green means "go." The child does not have to ask permission to do something. "Yellow" means, "Ask the teacher." This is a situation that can change from time to time. Red means "Stop!" Under no circumstances is the child to engage in the behavior. For example, there may be some times in the day you may want a quieter classroom. You can have a red traffic light by the pencil sharpener to indicate no sharpening of pencils during that time.

Strategy
107

Have a Feather Duster

Have a feather duster available. When a child comes in who is angry or in a bad mood, tell the child to dust his "angries" off until he feels better. This is a really simple and effective technique. You are teaching the child that it is okay to have the feeling of anger, but there is also a way to help feel better.

Strategy
108

Use the Powerful Tool of Music

Humans adapt biologically to what is going on rhythmically (Baker & Jones). For example, in a college dorm when music is playing, all students are in sync with the beat. Play calming music as children come into the classroom. Play calming music on days when children are feeling antsy. Calming music is music that has a slow rhythm. It is instrumental music with no words.

You can also use music to have the children move around. Play fun upbeat songs so that they will sing along.

Teach Self-Talk

Children can learn self-control when they say words to themselves when they are upset (Thelwell et al., 2006). When something upsetting happens, children generally tend to think, "I'm angry, " or "I can't handle this." Teach them positive words to say to themselves. Here are some examples.

Examples of Self-Talk
"I can do it." " I am okay." " I can handle this." " I don't have to stay angry."

Have a Calming Mat

A child may become angry and frustrated and need something special to help him calm down. Have a special large rug mat that is kept stored until needed. Tell children ahead of time that if they ever want to have a temper tantrum, they can go to the Calming Mat. Explain that you want them to be very safe when they do this, so you are providing them with a special mat for when they are angry and feel like having a tantrum. Tell them to ask you for it when they wish to use it.

This provides a space for children to kick and scream without a fuss from you. It teaches them that it is okay to be angry and upset without hurting someone else. This can prevent children from hitting or hurting someone else.

When the child is calmed down, the child returns the mat to you until someone else needs it.

Strategy
111

Have a Breathing Bell

Throughout the day, take breaks. Set a timer to go off at random times. When the buzzer goes off, everyone takes 3 deep breaths and then goes back to what they were doing. Deep breathing relieves stress and stimulates brain cells.

Have an "I Can" Can

This is a technique for children who tend to be negative. These are children who say, "I can't," or "It's too hard." Have a small can on which you have written the words, "I Can." Have the children draw pictures or write all the things they can do and put it all in the can. When they are feeling negative, have them get out their very own "I Can" Can and see all the things they can do. Each child has his own can.

Have the children add to their cans all new accomplishments.

Use an Options Statement

The options statement provides the child with alternatives. First cue the child by saying the child's name, so the child will listen to you.

When a child misbehaves, present two positive options. "Tanesha, you may go over to the Relaxation Station or you may go to the language center now." Be clear, concise, and concrete.

Have Mouse Pads

Some children need to move. They will tap their pencil continually or shake a foot. This gives them a way to move, without having them get up and down. They simply tap their finger on the mouse pad.

Strategy
115

Paradoxical Intervention

There are two effective, yet different ways to use this powerful intervention. The first method is excellent for power struggles. The goal is to give the child exactly what they seem to be demanding (Frankl, V.E., 1963). Once they have it, they no longer want it. Here is an example. Minetta is a first-grader. She daily asks her teacher to go to the nurse's office. It happens at exactly the same time, right after lunch. Daily, her teacher says to her, "Minetta," I really don't think you are sick. What is the problem?" All of this takes up valuable class time. Each day, the nurse sends Minetta back to her classroom saying nothing is wrong. The teacher is increasingly frustrated. Here's how the paradoxical intervention works for this problem. Just before 1:00, the teacher calls Minetta up to her desk to have a private moment. The teacher says, "I know you may not feel well today so I have prepared for you a pass to go to the nurse's office. As a matter of fact, I have one for each day this week." Minetta is shocked. She gets real quiet, and then she says to her teacher, "You know, today I feel better and don't need to go to the nurse's office."

The second method is effective for temper tantrums and other behavioral issues (Zarske, 1993). It is also paradoxical. The paradox in this case is that the child is asked to determine a solution for the problem. For example, in the case of temper tantrums, the child comes up with a place to go within the classroom prior to the tantrum, to calm down. This is extremely empowering for the child. When the child feels like having a temper tantrum, the child simply goes to that special place in the classroom for a pre-determined period of time (by the child), and then returns to join the classroom.

Strategy
116

Stop and Give Me 5

Teach the students five things to do when you say, "Stop and Give me 5." 1) Students look at you; 2) They close their mouths; 3) They raise 5 fingers of one hand; 4) They open their ears; 5) They stand absolutely still.

Strategy
117

The 2-Hand Rule

Every time students want to talk, they raise their hand. At the same time that the student raises one hand, the other hand covers the mouth. This is a reminder to not blurt out.

Strategy
118

Blurt Pad

Students like Johnny who want to frequently blurt out, are given a little pad of paper. It is called a Blurt Pad. Instead of blurting out, the child puts a mark on the blurt pad. It is the child's own reinforcement for not blurting out. The child is acknowledged at the end of the day for using the blurt pad instead of blurting out.

Silence Sign

Strategy
119

Hold up a special sign that says, "Silence." When the children see the sign, they all stop talking, look at you, stand still, and fold their arms in front of them.

To ensure this works, hold up the sign, and say to the children who are near you, "I like the way Michael sees the sign, and now, Jamie sees the sign....." naming children's names. Soon they will all see the sign and stop talking.

Power of Silence

Strategy
120

Use the power of silence. Follow behavioral directions with a pause, taking two breaths while maintaining direct eye contact.

Do NOT overreact. When you lose your composure in front of the class, they are in control of your behavior.

Develop selective hearing when you suspect that the student is trying to bait you.

How to Handle Power Struggles

Power struggles are common with children (Mendler, 1997). They are growing up and wanting to assert their own independence. First and foremost, remember that it takes at least two people to have a power struggle. When one person stops, the struggle is over. It is therefore important to know a fundamental rule of handling power struggles.

Strategy
121

Do Not Argue

When you argue with the child, you are automatically buying into the argument. There is no argument. There can be only one person in charge in a classroom, and it will either be you or it will be the child. The same is true in the home, it will either be the parent, or it will be the child. Children are not ready for that power. This does not mean that their input is not valued. However, the time for gathering input is prior to any struggle. It is during group meetings or one-to-one contact.

Delay Method

Strategy
122

Instead of addressing the issue while the child is upset, wait for a pause and calmly say, "Sounds like that is important to you. I'm glad that you have things that you feel strongly about. I will be glad to talk with you about it after class work is finished."

Two Positive Choices

Strategy
123

After you have used the Delay Method, provide two positive choices. "Now, you get to make a decision. You can complete your class work or you can work in the reading center. Which do you prefer?"

Startle Response

Strategy
124

Talk about something else that is interesting for the child. "Wow, I see you have new shoes."

Here is a quick quiz for you to check to see how much you learned. If there are some areas that are weak for you, re-read that section and take this quiz again when you are through. Get 100% every time so that you know you've really "got it!" Your children and you will both feel the effects of your new knowledge.

___ 1. Use the same discipline techniques for each situation.

___ 2. Momentum means going quickly.

___ 3. "The Look" needs to be mean and angry.

___ 4. If you shout across the room at a child, you are teaching yelling through role modeling.

___ 5. The logical consequence of spilling something is for the child to spill something else and to clean it up.

___ 6. When you pay attention to negative behaviors, you weaken them.

___ 7. It's perfectly okay to redirect the misbehaving child.

___ 8. Whatever you put your attention on, will decrease.

___ 9. The calming mat is used as a traffic signal.

___ 10. The traffic signal is used for tantrums.

___ 11. It takes only one person to have a power struggle.

___ 12. It is not okay to argue with a child even when the child is wrong.

1F; 2F; 3F; 4T; 5F; 6F; 7T; 8F; 9F; 10F; 11; 12T

Chapter **5**

HOW TO PREVENT DISCIPLINE PROBLEMS BEFORE THEY HAPPEN

Prevention is as important as discipline techniques. If you use the following methods, you will prevent problems before they ever happen.

Provide a Developmentally Appropriate Curriculum and Environment

Provide for the children's individual needs (Dunn & Kontos, 1997). It is important that you have a curriculum that will meet these needs. No two children are exactly alike. A developmentally appropriate curriculum takes this into account. It has a curriculum that is age and developmentally appropriate and that is stimulating and fun for children.

The environment needs to be geared toward children, not toward adults. It needs to meet the needs of each of the children so that no child feels frustrated and inept. It makes a statement without words. The statement is "You're important. This is your special place. I am glad you're here"

Strategy
126

Be a Positive Role Model

You are one of the most important people in your children's lives. You are a role model, a "teacher," an example for them at all times (MacIntyre, K., 1998). You are that role model simply because they are in your presence.

It's imperative that you "clean up your own act!" If you want peaceful, loving, and joyful children, then you need to be that way.

It's a sacred responsibility being in charge of children. It is not something that can be taken for granted. Children can learn behaviors that you dislike within yourself simply from watching you in action.

They are extremely intuitive. They can sense if something is going on in your life to make you unhappy. They may not know what the unhappiness is about, but they can "intuitively sense" your feelings. They know if you are calm. What is it that you really want to teach your children? Do you want them to learn to be calm and happy? Then, you have to start now to be that way.

Spend time with yourself. Learn to love yourself more and more. The more that you respect yourself, the more children will see that, and the more they will learn to respect you. They will copy you liking yourself. You will be that role model for them. If you are a generous and giving person, they will see that. If you can receive love easily from others, they will see that. Therefore, it's important to "be" what you want most for your children to be. You start it. It all begins with you.

Strategy
127

Explain Situations Ahead of Time

Children have the need to know in advance what is going to happen just as you do. The Table of Contents for this book shows you what will be covered. It's better than having to dig through the book to find out what is covered. There are no surprises. It's the same with children. They too, need to know what to expect.

Prepare children as much as possible for what is going to be happening in their lives. If there is going to be a major change, tell them. They don't have to know all of the details, but they need to know the details that will affect them. They can intuitively sense any potential changes anyhow.

Tell them about minor changes also. Are you going to be redecorating a room? Are you going to add a set of shelves? These may seem minor to you. To a child who needs order, that is a major change. Are you going to have visitors? Tell them that also.

Strategy
128

Provide Choices

Children have the need to be independent, yet they really want your

136

approval rather than disapproval (Pettig, K.L., 2000). If you will provide children with choices, they will feel independent and still be choosing behaviors that meet your approval.

The goal needs to be freedom within limits. Here's an example. Offer a child a choice of doing several kinds of jobs. You are in charge. You are naming the kinds of jobs that the child can have. The child is in charge of deciding which he or she wants. You are both empowered.

Do the same for other situations. Have fun involving and empowering children.

Have a Variety of Bad Weather Day Activities Available

Strategy
129

Children frequently misbehave just before the weather changes. Be ready for those special days, those days when children need more movement activities. Be on the look-out for new ideas and fun activities for children. Subscribe to book clubs. Go to bookstores. Create ideas from things that you see children discover.

Save an activity for that special day

when children are "antsy." Make sure that the activity doesn't take a lot of concentration. On those kinds of days, children will be more interested in movement, games, singing, and laughing.

Strategy
130

| Tell Children "Thank You" for Appropriate Behaviors |

Never let a day go by without thanking children for something that children said or did that is appropriate. You will be making a difference in children's lives. Thank and praise each individual child for something different.

Say thank you to children when they remember to do something that you have asked. Adults generally remember to remind children of the WRONG things that they do, but rarely speak about all of the things that they do that are RIGHT. Show your approval and love. Don't always attach the thank-you or praise to a behavior. Sometimes, attach it to the child's "beingness," just the fact that each child is in your life. Say words like, "I'm so glad you are here today. Thanks." Each child is so special. Each child brings you so much.

Other ways you can show children you are grateful for them include smiles and comments like "Good job,"... "Good choice,"..."I'm lucky to have you in my life."

It's important to be sincere when you speak to the children. They can sense it if you are not sincere.

Watch Diets of Children

Strategy
131

Diet can influence behavior. Avoid foods that have excessive amounts of sugar, carbohydrates, artificial food colors, and flavorings (Rogers & Morris, 1986). They can contribute to behavior problems.

Halloween can be a very difficult time because children eat so much "junk food." Be prepared. Have movement activities for after the holiday. Limit what children eat for this holiday and for other special events.

Check labels on the foods you serve. Be careful that children don't see you eat foods that you won't let them eat. Remember, you are a role model.

Strategy
132

Set Rules

Children need rules. They thrive when there are positive rules set. Start with just one rule. The first rule can be one about not running in the room. All rules need to be positively stated. For example, this rule can be stated, "We all walk in this room." Have a visual clip art of someone walking next to the rule.

The more involved the children are in setting the rules, the more likely it is that they will be followed (Cartwright, 2004). Have the rules posted somewhere where all students can see them.

Strategy
133

Have a Positive Attitude

Believe in yourself and in the children. Think positively all of the time. If you become negative and think of yourself as weak or unable to handle a situation, that is exactly what will happen. If you firmly and joyfully believe in yourself and your abilities, you will do a better job with the children.

140

Follow Through

When you say something, it is important to follow through. This will help children to always know what is going to happen. It is confusing for children to hear one thing, and then have it "change" later. They never know what to expect. It's important for children to feel secure. They need to be able to believe in you and your word. Then they will be able to respect you more.

Help children by always following through. Be consistent and provide the structure that children need so very much.

Foster Self-Esteem

Self-esteem is essential. The better that children feel about themselves, the better they will do, and the better they will be. Positive discipline and guidance fosters self-esteem in children. Punishment and NEGATIVE WORDS deplete self-esteem and confidence in children. Use caution with your words and attitudes towards children.

STRATEGIES TO FOSTER
SELF-ESTEEM

Here are some additional methods for fostering self-esteem in your children. Rank in order from "one through five" the ones you need to do more.

Strategy
136

Have a curriculum that is developmentally appropriate.

Strategy
137

Help each child be a problem solver.

Strategy
138

Show genuine interest in each child.

Strategy
139

Help each child to feel important, loved, and wanted.

Strategy
140

Allow children to do appropriate tasks independently.

Strategy
141

Respect each child's feelings.

Tell children their strengths.

Strategy
142

Give honest, sincere appreciation and praise for jobs well done.

Strategy
143

Make sure that each child feels he has accomplished something successfully each day.

Strategy
144

Praise improvement.

Strategy
145

Provide encouragement. "You can do it."

Strategy
146

Be truthful and sincere.

Strategy
147

Be tactful.

Strategy
148

Observe each child to determine his needs and modify where needed.

Strategy
149

Be a good listener.

Strategy
150

**Strategy
151**

Enjoy the children. They will sense it and thrive in your care.

WAYS TO CHANGE A CHILD'S SELF-IMAGE FROM NEGATIVE TO POSITIVE AND FOSTER SELF-ESTEEM

**Strategy
152**

Be Careful of What You Say

Children believe it when they hear they are bad.

**Strategy
153**

Have Realistic Expectations of Your Children

Do not expect too much or too little.

**Strategy
154**

Give the Gift of Time

Have a special time to talk to the child when you can focus all your attention on the child. Time is the most precious commodity we now have, more valuable than money. It is often what we give the least. It's easier to give a gift like a sticker. How do you feel when someone spends time with you? You feel important and cared for. Do this for your children.

Do Not Withhold Caring and Love as a Punishment.

Strategy 155

Use the Four Step Life Lesson

Strategy 156

Offer your child choices so the child can learn to solve his or her own problems. Try the "Four Step Life Lesson."

1. Teach the child how to handle a situation.

2. Practice the situation with the child.

3. Let the child handle it.

4. Discuss it afterwards letting the child tell you how she did, and thank child for positive behaviors.

Strategy
157

| Choose Your Words Carefully |

Be very careful of your words. Use no put-downs or negative labels even as a joke.

Strategy
158

| Help Each Child to Be a Good Friend to Others |

Strategy
159

| Teach Children to Ask for What They Need |

Teach children appropriate ways to be assertive and ask for what they need. Practice this with the children.

Strategy
160

| Give the Children Responsibilities |

Response-Plus-Able equals responsible. Make sure that the child is able to make the response, that it is not something too difficult for the child to do.

Smile Frequently

Strategy
161

Children want to be with someone that is happy and caring. A simple smile at appropriate times can help each child feel happier.

Smile when children do something that is appropriate. Smile when you greet children in the morning.

Your smile will help each child feel cared about and important.

Use Preventive Prompts

Strategy
162

These are calm reminders to prevent misbehavior. A preventive prompt can be words, *"Jerald, remember to stay calm like you practiced."* Another example of a preventive prompt can be a token or paper to give the child as a reminder to not engage in misbehavior.

Remove Seductive Objects

Strategy
163

There are some objects that children simply can't resist. Remove these from the room or place them in an out-of-the-way place.

Strategy 164

Have "2 or More" of Popular Objects

Sometimes children all want the same object. Have two or more of the most popular objects. This eliminates fighting over the object because there are more objects, and they all get to use them.

Strategy 165

Speak Positively to Students

Some children may appear to have "thick skin," yet they are affected by everything that is said to them. As a matter of fact, sometimes, the "thick skin" is just a cover-up for insecurity. The damage can be devastating in terms of their esteem. Remember, that once a word has been spoken, it can never be taken back.

Sometimes, things said with the best intentions, can still be hurtful. Here are some other ways to talk to children. Look at the incorrect way, and then see the difference by looking at the correct way.

INCORRECT STATEMENTS
"Be careful. That's sloppy." "That is wrong."

CORRECT STATEMENTS
"Let me show you another way to do this." "Here is another way to do that."

Avoid Criticism

Strategy
166

It is better to say nothing at all than to use criticism. Criticism "puts-down" a child. Your goal is to always "put-up" your children.

Remember that Once a Word has Been Spoken, It Can Never be Taken Back.

Strategy
167

Here are some words and phrases that are "put-ups" that can brighten a child's day when they are sincerely said.

Words

Congratulations	Incredible
Super	Great
Outstanding	Fantastic
Terrific	Excellent
Wonderful	Marvelous
Perfect	Fine
Tremendous	Wow
Good	Sensational
Superb	Right
Correct	Beautiful
Unbelievable	Exciting
Exactly	Astonishing
Awesome	Nice

Phrases

That's fantastic.
I believe in you.
I knew you could do it.
You're doing fine.
That's so fine.
That's the way.
Much better.
You can do it.
Now you've got the hang of it.
You remembered.
Right on.
You're doing a good job.
I like that.
You really worked hard.
Thank you for being here.
Good answer.
You don't miss anything.
You must be proud of yourself.
You figured that one out.
Glad you are here today.

References

American Psychiatric Association. (2000). Diagnostic and statistical manual of mental disorders DSM-IV-TR (Text Revision). Washington, DC: Author.

Anguiaro, P. (2001). A first-year teacher's plan to reduce misbehavior in the classroom. Teaching Exceptional Children, 33(3), 52-56.

Appelbaum, M. (2006). How to Handle the Hard to Handle Student. Houston, TX: Appelbaum Training Institute.

Appelbaum, M. (1997). Do It Right, A Positive Guide to Discipline. Houston, TX: Appelbaum Training Institute.

Appelbaum, M. (1999). How to Listen so Kids will Talk. Houston, TX: Appelbaum Training Institute.

Armstrong, S. & Rentz, T. (2002). Improving listening skills and motivation. Eric ED468085.

Baker, F. & Jones, C. (2006). The effect of music therapy services on classroom behaviors of newly arrived refugee students in Australia: A pilot study. Emotional and Behavioural Difficulties, 11(4), 249-260.

Belfiore, P.J., Lee, D.L., Sheeler, M.C., & Klein, D. (2002). Implications of behavior momentum and academic achievement for students with behavior disorders: Theory, application, and practice. Psychology in the Schools, 39(2), 171-180.

Biederman, J., Petty, C., Hirshfeld-Becker, D.R., Henin, A., Faraone, S.V., Dang, D., Jakubowski, A., & Rosenbaum, J. (2006). A controlled longitudinal 5 year follow-up study of children at high and low risk for panic disorder and major depression. Psychological Medicine, 36(8), 1141-1152.

Bober, D. & Martin, A. (2006). Understanding anxiety disorders in children and adolescents: Brief overview and update. Psychiatric Times, 23(3), 10-16.

Brazelton, T.B., Greenspan, S.I., (2001). The irreducible *needs* of *children*: What every child musthave to grow, learn, and flourish. New York, NY: Perseus Books

Buffum, A. & Hinman, C. (2006). Professional learning communities: Reigniting passion and purpose. Leadership, 35(5), 16-19.

Burnham, J.J., Schaefer, B.A., & Giesen, J. (2006). An empirical taxonomy of youths' fears: Cluster analysis of the American fear survey schedule. Psychology in the Schools, 43(6), 673-683.

Carlson, F.M. & Nelson, B.G. (2006). Reducing aggression with touch. Dimensions of Early Childhood, 34(3), 9-15.

Cartwright, S. 2004. Teachers on teaching. Young citizens in the making. Young Children 59 (5): 108-109.

Cavanagh, S.E. & Huston, A.C. (2006). Family instability and children's early problem behavior. Social Forces, 85(1), 551-581.

Curwin, R.L. & Mendler, A.N. (1988). Discipline with Dignity. Alexandria, VA: Association for Supervision and Curriculum Development.

De Montigny, F., & Lacharite, C. (2005). Perceived parental efficacy: Concept analysis. Journal of Advanced Nursing, 49(4), 387-396.

Dunn, L. & Kontos, S. (1997). Research in review: What have we learned about developmentally appropriate practice. Young Children, 52(5), 4-13.

Frankle, V.E. (1963). Man's search for meaning: An introduction to logotherapy. Boston, MA: Beacon Press.

Frederickson, N., Warren, L., & Turner, J. (2005). Circle of friends: An exploration of impact over time. Educational Psychology in Practice, 21(3), 197-217.

Greenburg, P. (2005). Setting limits: When a child overwhelms and controls, 19(7), 14-16.

Grossman, D., & DeGaetano, G. (1999). *Stop Teaching Our Kids to Kill: A Call to Action Against TV*, Movie and Video Game Violence, New York, NY: Crown Books (Random House).

Higa, C.K., Fernandez, S.N., Nakamura, B. J., Chorpita, B.F., Daleiden, E.L. (2006).

Parental Assessment of Childhood Social Phobia: Psychometric Properties of the Social Phobia and Anxiety Inventory for Children–Parent Report. Journal of Clinical Child & Adolescent Psychology, 35(4), 590-597.

Hofferth, Sandra L. . Healthy Environments , Healthy Children: Children in Families. . Ann Arbor, MI: Institute for Social Research; 1998.

Kane,R.G., Maw, N. (2005). Making sense of learning at secondary school: Involving students to improve teaching practice. Cambridge Journal of Education, 35(3), 311-322.

Kanevsky, L., Keighley,T. (2003). To produce or not to produce? Understanding boredom and honor in underachievement, Roeper Review, 26(1), 20-28.

Kayale, K.A. & Forness, S.R. (1995). The nature of learning disabilities: Critical elements of diagnosis and classification. Mahwah, NJ: Lawrence Erbaum Associates.

Laursen, E.K. (2003). Principle-centered discipline. Reclaiming Children & Youth, 12(2), 78-83.

MacIntyre, K. (1998). When opposites attract: Using differences to make a difference. Young Children, 53(5), 84-84.

Mash, E.J., Wolfe, D.A. 2002. Abnormal child psychology. (2nd ed.). Belmont, CA: Wadsworth Thomson Learning.

Maughan, A., Cicchetti,D. (2002). Impact of child maltreatment and interadult violence on children's emotion regulation abilities and socioemotional adjustment. Child Development (73(5), 1525-1567.

Mayeux, L., Cillessen, A. (2003). Development of social problem solving in early childhood: Stability, change, and associations with social competence. Journal of Genetic Psychology, 164(2), 153-174.

Mendler, A.N. (1997). Power Struggles, Successful Techniques for Educators. Minneapolis, MN: Free Spirit Publishing.

McIntosh, B.J. (1989). Spoiled child syndrome. Pediatrics, 83(1), 108-116.

Mierzwik, D. (2004). *Quick and easy ways to connect with students and their parents.* Thousand Oaks, CA: Corwin Press.

Ostrov, J.M., Gentile, D.A., & Crick, N.R. (2006). Media exposure, aggression and prosocial behavior during early childhood: A longitudinal study. Social Development, 15(4), 612-627.

Papneja, T., Manassis, K. (2006). Characterization and treatment responses of anxious children with asthma. Canadian Journal of Psychiatry, 51(6), 393-396.

Passe, J. (1996). When students choose content: A guide to increasing motivation, autonomy, and achievement. Thousand Oaks, CA: Corwin Press.

Pettig, K.L. (2000). On the road to differentiated practice. Educational Leadership, 58(1), 14-18.

Poole, C., Miller, S.A., Church, E.B. (2004). Development: Ages & stages: How self-concept develops. Early Childhood Today, 3 (19), 31-35.

Prestia, K. (2004). Incorporate sensory activities and choices into the classroom. Intervention in School & Clinic, 39.

Rodale, A. (2006). Overworked and overbooked. Prevention, 58(10), 212-212.

Rogers, C.S., & S. S. Morris. 1986. Reducing sugar in children's diets: How? why? Young Children, 41(5): 11-16.

Roosevelt, F.D. (1932). Baltimore address. Recovered from internet 12/11/06 http://www.presidency.ucsb.edu/ws/index.php?pid=15280

Ruffman, T. (1999). Children's understanding of logical inconsistency. Child Development, 70(4), 872-887.

Rutherford, R.B., Mathur, S.R. & Schoenfeld, N.A. (2006). Severe behavior disorders of children and youth: Introduction. Education & Treatment of Children, 29(4), 529-532.

Schwarz, G. (1989). The teacher. Educational Leadership, 46(5), 82-84.

Silsbee, D. (2005). Cultivating classroom authenticity. Education Digest, 71(1), 14-16.

Tanner, B.M., Bottoms, G., Feagin, C., Beaman, A. (2003). Instructional strategies: How teachers teach matters. Southern Regional Education Board, 1-44.

Thelwell, R., Greenlees, I, & Weston, N. (2006). Using psychological skills training to develop soccer performance. Journal of Applied Sport Psychology, 18(3), 254-270.

Tipps, C. (2006). Kids at hope: All children are capable of success—no exceptions! Journal of Physical Education, Recreation & Dance, 77(1), 24-26.

Valore, T.G., Cantrell, R.P. & Cantrell, M.L. (2006). Competency building in the context of groups. Reclaiming Children & Youth, 14(4), 228-235.

Wallace, L.B. (1993). Helping Children Cope with Violence. Young Children, 48(4), 4-11.

Wartella, E. (1999). Children and media: On growth and gaps. Mass Communication & Society, 2(1), 81-89.

Wilford, S. (2006). Policies and practices: Collaboration—Who are we as role models? Early Childhood Today, 20(6), 12-13.

Zarske, John A. (1993). A paradoxical intervention to reduce tantrums. In J.J. Cohen and M.C. Fish (Ed.), *Handbook of school-based interventions: Resolving student problems and promoting healthy educational environments* (85-86). San Francisco, CA: Jossey-Bass Publishing.

Index

H

I

L

M

N

O